Teach a Man to Fish

Engaging the Local Church to
Create Sustainable, Transformational Missions

TEACH A MAN
TO FISH

FLORENCE MUINDI MD
CHARLIE VITTITOW DMD
WITH JOSEPH & KATHLEEN SINDORF

Visit Tyndale online at tyndale.com.

Visit Life In Abundance International online at lifeinabundance.org.

Tyndale and Tyndale's quill logo are registered trademarks of Tyndale House Ministries.

Teach a Man to Fish: Engaging the Local Church to Create Sustainable, Transformational Missions

Copyright © 2024 by Florence Muindi and Charlie Vittitow. All rights reserved.

Cover and interior illustration of abstract fish copyright © Twins Design Studio/Shutterstock. All rights reserved.

Cover and interior illustration of background by Eva M. Winters. Copyright © Tyndale House Ministries. All rights reserved.

Interior illustration of church icon copyright © by IconPacks. All rights reserved.

Designed by Eva M. Winters

Unless otherwise indicated, all Scripture quotations are from The ESV® Bible (The Holy Bible, English Standard Version®), copyright © 2001 by Crossway, a publishing ministry of Good News Publishers. Used by permission. All rights reserved.

Scripture quotations marked KJV are taken from the *Holy Bible*, King James Version.

Scripture quotations marked NASB are taken from the (NASB®) New American Standard Bible,® copyright © 1960, 1971, 1977, 1995, 2020 by The Lockman Foundation. All rights reserved. www.lockman.org.

Scripture quotations marked NIV are taken from the Holy Bible, *New International Version,*® *NIV.*® Copyright © 1973, 1978, 1984, 2011 by Biblica, Inc.® Used by permission. All rights reserved worldwide.

Scripture quotations marked NLT are taken from the *Holy Bible*, New Living Translation, copyright © 1996, 2004, 2015 by Tyndale House Foundation. Used by permission of Tyndale House Publishers, Carol Stream, Illinois 60188. All rights reserved.

The URLs in this book were verified prior to publication. The publisher is not responsible for content in the links, links that have expired, or websites that have changed ownership after that time.

The events and conversations in this book have been recounted to the best of the authors' recollection. Some names, identities, and locations have been changed to protect individuals' privacy and safety.

For information about special discounts for bulk purchases, please contact Tyndale House Publishers at csresponse@tyndale.com, or call 1-855-277-9400.

Library of Congress Cataloging-in-Publication Data

A catalog record for this book is available from the Library of Congress.

ISBN 978-1-4964-9006-3

Printed in the United States of America

30	29	28	27	26	25	24
7	6	5	4	3	2	1

To Festus Muindi and Sherry Burnett Vittitow,
the Lord's greatest gifts to us, and our number one intercessors.

To the long lineage of elders at Southeast Christian Church
who had the vision to unleash the church.

And to our teammates at Life In Abundance International and
SECC whom we've had the high honor of serving alongside.

Table of Contents

Foreword

I was born on the mission field to Christian missionary parents. My father, Nate, was a missionary pilot working with a team to reach the Huaorani people of Ecuador. He and four of his missionary friends were martyred there in 1956. Ever since, my life has been inescapably linked to missions. I support missions financially, and I have been a missionary myself. I've also spent a lifetime observing missionary efforts, from both the sending and receiving ends, in more than fifty countries. I've seen what works and what doesn't work in the church's attempts to reach the world with the gospel. My work has also opened doors for me to meet some of the people God is using in his global mission.

I first met Charlie Vittitow, a dentist with a great deal of experience in dental outreaches through short-term missions, at a Global Missions Health Conference at Southeast Christian Church (SECC) in Louisville, Kentucky. As Charlie's work shifted from directly providing dental services to training local leaders in dental skills, he and I teamed up to develop a dental training system that could be used by indigenous Christians in frontier areas of the world to open the door to Christ's gospel.

At a subsequent Global Missions Health Conference, I was sitting in the second row among several thousand attendees when a Kenyan medical doctor, Florence Muindi, was introduced as our plenary speaker. Her voice was as soft as her stature was small, but her message was powerful! While listening to Florence speak, I began taking pages and pages of hurried notes. My wife, Ginny, was perplexed, not knowing why I was writing so furiously, and she wondered whether I was even paying attention. But I was completely immersed in Florence's message and didn't want to miss a word she said. I hardly had time to look up as Florence gave her testimony about how she and her ministry follow Christ's example by meeting the felt needs of hurting people and sharing the gospel with them. Her ministry, Life In Abundance International (LIA), now serves in fourteen countries in Africa and the Caribbean and sponsors an annual global missions conference in Kenya.

Florence grew up in Kenya, I grew up in Ecuador, and Charlie grew up in the United States. The three of us are very different—different culturally, different by training, and equipped with different spiritual gifts—but what we have in common is our commission from Jesus Christ to use our gifts, our training, our resources, and our opportunities to "go and make disciples of all nations . . . teaching them to obey everything [Jesus has] commanded."[1]

In 1 Corinthians 12, the apostle Paul makes it clear that individual Christ followers have been given various gifts by the Holy Spirit, and they are intended to function together. "The human body has many parts, but the many parts make up one whole body. So it is with the body of Christ."[2] That helps to explain how Charlie, Florence, and I are connected, though we come from such different settings.

God has promised that "everyone who calls on the name of the LORD will be saved."[3] But as Paul asks in the book of Romans,

How can they call on him to save them unless they believe in him? And how can they believe in him if they have never heard about him? And how can they hear about him unless someone tells them? And how will anyone go and tell them without being sent? That is why the Scriptures say, "How beautiful are the feet of messengers who bring good news!"[4]

Teach a Man to Fish will open your eyes to biblical principles that will inform the way you go about fulfilling your role in that commission, and it will introduce you to a strategy that I have seen bring forth lasting results in some of the most difficult places in the world.

Steve Saint
Founder, Indigenous People's Technology
and Education Center (ITEC)

Preface

FLORENCE

You've probably heard the saying, "Give a man a fish, and you feed him for a day. Teach a man to fish, and you feed him for a lifetime." The immediate gratification of a free fish is only a good and just option if the people are starving and need some quick emergency nutrition to prolong their lives. But as soon as the initial crisis has passed, the free fish program (relief) must stop so that the people can be taught the skills to become self-sufficient and feed themselves and others (development). We would all agree that learning new skills in order to have a lifetime supply of food is the preferable option.

This book is our love offering to the global church—for anyone who desires to serve in ways that honor God and produce lasting fruit. As you learn these principles and put them into practice, we pray they will pay eternal dividends and that God will be glorified. In the years ahead, we hope you'll be able to look back and see your work continuing to flourish.

In these pages, I share my very life with you, describing the journey the Lord has led me on and how he has taught me, enabled me, and brought me to a place where I can share these stories and principles with confidence, so that you also may be equipped to serve God wherever he leads you.

You will see God's kindness in how he invites each of us to serve him, and how he begins to mold us and equip us to fulfill the mission to which he has called us. God's kindness transforms us so we can become his agents of transformation.

I hope you will be inspired to serve God with confidence, knowing that the work you do is work that he approves. I believe you already want to serve God, not waste your life doing something that won't last or bear good fruit. But you may be wondering *how*.

How do I go about it?

Where do I begin?

What have others done successfully, and how has their work made a difference?

From our own experience, Charlie and I will show you that if you're willing to follow God's direction, your work will bear fruit. We've made some mistakes in the past that we hope you won't have to repeat. You can learn from our experiences and perhaps avoid some of the same pitfalls along the way.

Our prayer is that God will unleash something new and fresh in your life that will ripple out to the nations.

CHARLIE

We have sensed an urgency to finish our work and get this book into your hands. Together we must reach those who have not yet heard about Jesus Christ. And if the way we've been going about that task isn't working very well to achieve the desired results, then we must rediscover the biblical principles that will enable us to be more effective.

The personal stories and Kingdom principles we share here have all grown out of our own walk with Jesus Christ. We pray that they will take root and flourish in your life as well.

Serving with Florence on multiple mission fields, I've come to realize how much the body of Christ needs for every part of the body to function well—not for their own sake, but for the glory of God.

From the point of view of the American church, we may think

we've already got it all figured out. We have our missions programs; we're sending people out, both long-term and short-term; we're investing in overseas missions organizations and supporting missionaries in the US and abroad. I'm writing to my own tribe, the American church, to say that there is a way to develop cross-cultural partnerships that are more effective, more sustainable, and more fruitful than the traditional methods have been, and it's not as hard as you might think.

What do Christians from other nations have to offer the American church? That's what we want to show you. It's time for the whole body of Christ, on every continent, to learn how to function better *together*. It's time to invest all the resources we have in ways that will produce good fruit for generations to come.

Jesus told a parable about a man who went into a field and found a treasure—and then he sold everything he had to buy that field. The treasure had been there for a long time, but no one had discovered it; it had been neglected. When the man realized the value of it, he invested everything he had in order to claim it.

The treasure we're about to reveal is not a new revelation. It has been part of God's heart from the very beginning. Our hope is that you will rediscover these truths and claim the treasure that has been waiting for you!

With so many people across the globe who still don't know the name of Jesus, who still have yet to hear the gospel, the task before us is great. It's time for a renewed vision, a renewed motivation, and a renewed focus on reaching the world for Christ. And there's no better time than now to get started.

HOW WE LEARNED CROSS-CULTURAL PARTNERSHIP

LET'S GO TOGETHER

If you want to go fast, go alone;
if you want to go far, go together.
AFRICAN PROVERB

For the body does not consist of one member but of many.
1 CORINTHIANS 12:14

FLORENCE

When Charlie and I arrived in Port-au-Prince, Haiti, in 2011, the city was still digging out from a devastating earthquake that had destroyed much of the capital and the surrounding region the previous year.

This massive 7.0 earthquake had shaken the ground violently, and within moments hundreds of thousands of buildings collapsed into huge piles of rubble and twisted steel. More than one million Haitians were displaced, most of them rendered homeless. An estimated 300,000 died.[1]

As people from nations around the world began to respond, hundreds of tons of emergency relief were delivered to the devastated region and millions of dollars were raised within a few days.

At the time, Charlie was the missions pastor at Southeast Christian Church (SECC) in Louisville, Kentucky. Other leaders of the church wanted to take immediate action and make a dramatic response to this immense humanitarian crisis. Hundreds of generous people said they were willing to donate and join short-term missions (STM) teams to travel without delay to Haiti and help wherever they could.

But this wasn't Charlie's first time dealing with a natural disaster. He cautiously advised the church leaders to wait, knowing that the immediate need for emergency relief would be well-funded by governments and large-scale fundraising efforts. Help from the people of the church would be needed later for the rebuilding and development phase.

The Power of Unity

We had learned from experience that God blesses our work when we partner with local churches in disaster areas; and at the time of the 2010 earthquake, neither of us had any local church partners in Haiti. So Charlie assembled an initial survey team to travel to Haiti, investigate the need, visit the local churches, spend time in prayer, and listen for God's direction before trying to determine what the best response might be. When he invited me to join the team, his request was simple and straightforward: "Florence, let's go to Haiti and see what God is doing there. Let's go hear him together."

I am a Kenyan medical doctor with a specialty in public health. I've worked with child survival programs among the refugee populations in East Africa, with community health centers among the nomadic Maasai people in Kenya and Tanzania, and with those suffering with leprosy in Ethiopia.[2] As the founder and president of Life In Abundance, I've learned much about transformational community development, especially living and working in Nairobi, Kenya, home to the two largest urban slums in Africa.

Charlie and I had met a few years prior to 2010 in Kabul, Afghanistan, and we had worked together many times on projects in various countries before the Haitian earthquake. Time and again, our two organizations—LIA and SECC—had united in response to problems stemming most often from poverty.

We consistently found ourselves in agreement in our desire to see lasting transformation come to places of dependency and great need. We also agreed on the steps needed for this long-term change to take place. We had seen those steps implemented through local churches, and we knew it was a well-tested model that *worked*.

We formed our partnership by undertaking some seemingly impossible projects together in some very difficult places. Amid those challenging circumstances, we built a solid foundation for our relationship—trusting, testing that trust, and then finding the faith to trust even more. Ultimately, our joint experience became a testimony to the power of *unity*. Through it all, we discovered the truth of what David declares in Psalm 133: "How good and pleasant it is when God's people live together in unity! . . . For there the LORD bestows his blessing, even life forevermore."[3] When God's people are truly united, he blesses their work. It was clear that Haiti, and the church in Haiti, needed a blessing.

Don't Go It Alone

As individuals, we all have blind spots. In the words of an African proverb, "Nobody can see the back of their own head." But when we go into a new situation together with a trusted partner—as we did when we went into Haiti—our partner can see things we would miss on our own. During our time in Haiti, we were accompanied by a trusted colleague who knew Haiti well and was able to introduce us to people and organizations with whom he had established relationships.

Paul makes it clear in 1 Corinthians 12 that we are incomplete by ourselves. Using the metaphor of a human body, with each person representing a different part of the body, he says that God's people need to work together to increase their effectiveness. If we were to have any hope of making a lasting difference in Haiti, we knew it would require a full complement of knowledge, insight, skills, and abilities. By choosing to partner with local churches in Haiti, we created a situation in which our individual gifts and abilities were united, creating a synergy that resulted in far greater effectiveness. Together, we were much stronger than if we had tried to go it alone.

The situation we walked into in Haiti was still desperate, even a year after the devastating earthquake. But that was no surprise. Haiti has developed a reputation as a bottomless pit for relief money and a black hole for international aid. Despite billions upon billions of dollars spent to help this nation of just under 12 million people, Haiti is still an island of appallingly desperate poverty in a sea of comparatively wealthy neighbor nations.

Its most prosperous neighbor—the United States—is only seven hundred miles away, and that proximity makes the situation in Haiti seem even more desperate. On top of that, Americans have a propensity for trying to fix problems quickly, often by throwing money at them. But this is not the kind of help that Haiti truly needs.

We had learned that 60 percent of the Haitian population lives on less than two dollars per day. And one out of four Haitians lives in *extreme* poverty—on less than $1.25 per day. Half the children in Haiti do not attend school, and of those who do, about 30 percent drop out before the third grade, and 60 percent before the sixth grade. Less than half of the country's rural population has access to drinkable water, and only 25 percent of Haitians have access to basic sanitation.[4]

This horrific situation isn't because of a lack of worldwide concern or financial assistance. Haiti received $13 billion in foreign aid from the international community from 2011 to 2021,[5] but there is very little evidence that it helped improve the lives of the Haitian people.

Charlie and I were not blind to the overwhelming needs in Haiti, but when he said, "Would you go to Haiti with me to hear God together?" he meant exactly that. Not, "Let's go *take action*," but rather, "Let's go *pray, listen, wait,* and *observe . . .*"

Oddly, although Charlie works with ministries around the globe, and my ministry, Life In Abundance, operates in fourteen nations, neither of us had ever been to Haiti. This was unknown territory for us.

But we believed that God had not turned his back on the people of Haiti and that his work there was not yet finished. We wanted to hear whether he had a role for us in his plan. We simply desired to discern the heart of God. We both believed that if we prayed and sought God's guidance, he would direct us. We believed that God still speaks today, and if he had something to say to us about Haiti, we didn't want to miss it.

I wasn't planning to get involved in any hands-on projects; my ministry plate was already overflowing. Instead, the trip to Haiti for me was like going into a forest, noticing a large fallen tree, and wondering what would become of it. Would it be used to build a fire, cut into lumber at a mill and used to build a shelter, carved into a fine artistic work, or simply allowed to decompose into the soil?

Charlie and I had no preconceived ideas about what the outcome of our trip would be. We had no plan, except to go and hear what God had to say. We would see what the Great Creator would do with that broken tree—and we were excited to watch and celebrate it together.

Heartbreaking First Impressions

When we arrived in Haiti and traveled from the airport through the capital, we saw a shocking number of displaced people still living in flimsy tents and shacks. Buildings that had collapsed during the earthquake were still piles of rubble, the streets were lined with trash, and debris was piled everywhere. UNICEF confirmed what we were seeing. They estimated that, one year after the disaster, "more than one million people remain displaced, living in crowded camps where livelihoods, shelter and services are still hardly sufficient for children to stay healthy."[6]

The time for emergency relief for the survivors of the earthquake was well past, but well-meaning international organizations were still providing it. We knew from experience how vitally important it is to move on quickly from emergency relief to restoration and development; otherwise, for the victims, outside aid replaces self-sufficiency with a destructive dependence on external sources of food, shelter, and other essentials of life.

We saw countless humanitarian agencies busily operating relief centers and running various programs and activities, and we wondered how anyone could ever hope to empower the Haitian people to forsake years of dependence on free aid and take ownership of their own development. How could any program or organization help to restore their dignity and self-sufficiency, and transform their lives to a level they could sustain?

When someone from America, or any other comparatively rich nation, goes into an impoverished country such as Haiti and asks, "What are your needs?" the question may arise from a genuine compassionate desire to help. But from the receiver's perspective, it's an intimidating question—in fact, it might even feel like an interrogation. Feeling pressured to admit your inability to properly care for your own family is both degrading and demeaning to a person. And what's worse, when the foreigners eventually, and inevitably, depart, the hopeful recipients are usually left disappointed, with their felt needs still largely unmet.

We have found that the only way to break this vicious cycle is by establishing our development efforts through cooperative partnerships with local people who will still be active and vital in the community long after we've gone home.

So Where Was the Local Church?

As we continued to observe and pray about what we were seeing, we couldn't help but wonder, *Where is the Haitian church?* Life In Abundance will not enter a community to help with development without the active involvement of the local churches. Likewise, one of Southeast Christian Church's operating principles is to only work with programs that are connected to local churches.

It's not as if there were no Haitians at all serving their communities in a godly way; but it was understandably difficult for local farmers to compete against free food or for a local doctor to provide health care when the people could get their health care for free . . . at least for a season. With all the billions of dollars of international aid being disbursed throughout the country, Charlie and I frankly wondered whether we would be able to find any local churches who had the desire to stop benefiting from the relief efforts and who would take a lead role in the development of their community.

Though we were concerned, it was important to remember that the leaders and members of the local Haitian churches were our brothers and sisters in Christ—not some strangers or "poor people" we were there to rescue. We try never to go into a community from a position of power or prestige, or promising things we can't provide. Our desire is always to build interdependent partnerships based on humility and the desire to see God glorified. We feel strongly that any relationship we enter into must be one in which God is exalted through the local church.

Discovering My Own People

As we kept our ears tuned to hear God's voice, I was also keeping my eyes open to discover whatever resources already existed in the communities we were visiting. In one particular Haitian village, I noticed a particular type of bean growing there. These same beans are peculiar to the area in Kenya where I grew up. We call them pigeon peas, and they are a staple of our diet.

That observation stayed in my mind because through all my extensive international travels, I had never seen pigeon peas growing anywhere else. Yet here they were in Haiti. It totally surprised me.

I also began to notice other things this village had in common with my tribe—little things, such as the way they stacked their charcoal and how they roasted and sold corn on the streets. Moreover, the people there practiced voodoo—much like my Kenyan tribe, which is known for witchcraft. There were so many similarities that I thought, *These could be my people. I wonder if we actually have common roots.*

All those familiar characteristics gave me a sense that I might be in this region of Haiti for a reason. As an African, I began to feel I had a responsibility to help the local believers discover how to deal with the voodoo powers in their midst. While this is still uncharted territory for much of the Western church, churches in Africa have learned how to deal with spiritual warfare—including taking authority over the powers of witchcraft—and we have been waging war in the spirit realm for centuries.

As I continued to notice the parallels between my African tribe and this village in Haiti, I began to wrestle with a fundamental question: *How can the global church help the Haitian church?* And on a very personal level, I wondered, *As I continue to bring sustainable development to the poor and vulnerable in Africa, how can I do nothing here, now that I see that I might have a historical connection with these people?*

When we visited the home of a local pastor, the Lord convicted me in a powerful way, and I understood that these villagers were where they are today because of what Africans had done in the past. My forefathers could have been among those who played a role in enslaving the forefathers of these Haitians—or at least allowed that travesty to take place. They are still enslaved today, both economically and spiritually—no longer in physical chains, perhaps, but bound by poverty, evil powers, learned helplessness, and the loss of their dignity.

I broke down and wept with the realization that the people I'd met here might have been part of my tribe, and that my own people may have contributed to their poverty and bondage. It was a gut-wrenching, intuitive response that shook me to the core.

I realized, too, that I—and by extension, Life In Abundance—had a responsibility to bring transformation and healing to this village. We had a role to play that could not be filled by Americans in quite the same way as it could be done by Africans. It had become very clear to me that we shared the blame, we shared responsibility, and we must also share in working for a solution.

We Asked and God Answered

Charlie could see that I was moved emotionally, and as we prepared to fly home, we stopped by a river that flows into that small Haitian town. We prayed there together, asking God to show us what to do next. We both believed that God had brought things to our attention, during our days in this village, that made us realize he had roles we could fill—roles that neither Africans nor Americans could take on alone. We had to go together. Having come to that realization, we recognized that the next step would be to find local churches that had a burden for their people and a desire to partner with us in bringing long-lasting change to their communities.

Little did we know, when we stopped to pray by that river, that we were standing in the backyard of the church that was to become the leader—and a model for other churches—in turning things around in that region. Over the next three and a half years, something unheard of happened in that part of Haiti: nothing short of *transformation*! Physical, material, and spiritual changes took hold, and the development projects continued to grow, fully sustained by the local community. This was almost unprecedented in Haiti.

Hebrews 11:1 tells us that "faith is the assurance of things hoped for," and by faith we entered into the next phase of our work there. Looking at the many examples of failed development projects throughout the region, we knew we could not rely on our own knowledge or strategy; we had to rely on God. Our hope was founded on his love for the Haitian people, and by faith we had full assurance that he would lead us. And he did.

Our first project on the island was a real success, and we'll tell you more about it later in the book—how local churches, like the one by the river, took ownership for leading the development of their communities. And we'll tell you what's happening in that village today. The transformation there has indeed been miraculous, and God has received all the glory.

Charlie and I have worked together in many partnerships around the world, both before and after Haiti. Together, we have a history of decades of prayer and the transformative action that grew out of answers to those prayers. What we have learned has given birth to biblical principles that guide our work in helping communities rise out of poverty and find abundant life in Jesus Christ. We're eager to share with you some of the knowledge and wisdom we have acquired along the way.

Our prayer is that God will breathe life into these words and that you will be inspired. As you look for ways to apply these principles to your own situation, we pray that you will find like-minded partners, and that together your labors for God will produce a bountiful harvest so that he will get all the glory.

Questions for Reflection and Journaling

1. How does the story of our work in Haiti relate to your own experience? Can you remember a time when you weren't sure what God wanted you to do, but you took the next step that seemed right? What signs did you see of God's faithfulness and guidance during that time?

2. Is there a time you remember being certain of God's leading? What direction did he give you then?

3. How are you listening for God's leading in your life right now?

EIGHTY-FIVE PEOPLE WE CAN'T HELP!

Progress is impossible without change;
and those who cannot change their minds cannot change anything.
GEORGE BERNARD SHAW

What you have heard from me in the presence of many witnesses
entrust to faithful men, who will be able to teach others also.
2 TIMOTHY 2:2

CHARLIE

The last day of any short-term missions trip is always the most challenging, especially if you've spent hours every day working in people's mouths, relieving dental pain by extracting abscessed teeth.

Word gets out from the patients who were seen during the first few days, and that word-of-mouth promotion results in a steady stream of people arriving—each one hoping to see a dentist and have their pain taken away before we leave.

Having been on many short-term medical missions trips, I know I must be prepared to hit the ground running when we arrive at a location to set up our clinic. Usually there are hundreds of people already waiting who have heard that free dental care is available, and many have traveled a very long way to get help. For some, this will be their first-ever visit to a dentist—and they all need it very badly.

During the entire week of the clinic, the work never slows down. The patients just keep coming. The makeshift clinic looks like total chaos, but it's actually well-organized into stations of triage, treatment, sterilization, and prayer. Many of those heading to the dental chair have an especially high interest in prayer!

Back in the 1990s, before battery-powered headlamps were available, the dental chair would often be set up facing an open window in order to get enough light. As you can imagine, the patients who were waiting their turn would crowd outside the window to watch. Knowing their turn would come, these curious observers were keen to assess the process and the skills of the providers. Many times, in the middle of a procedure, the light would suddenly disappear—blocked by too many spectators.

Such trips were always very fruitful, fulfilling, and *exhausting*. It was wonderful to see the suffering of hundreds of people relieved, and they were all incredibly grateful. A short-term team is happy to invest a week of their time serving a poor community where dental problems are just one of many serious challenges people face on a daily basis. The local churches that host the clinics are able to meet people from their community—many of whom have had no previous exposure to the church—and minister to them in their pain and time of need.

The small local churches that hosted our teams were able to experience the same powerful connection between physical health and receptivity to the gospel that Jesus modeled throughout his own earthly ministry. We saw the hearts of patients and their families open to Jesus as they experienced the compassion and love of Christ through this faithful team of believers working together.

The Trip That Changed Everything

In the summer of 2003, a dental team from our church, which included my family, was wrapping up another week of serving alongside a church in a poor community in Jamaica. It was the last day of the clinic, and within an hour we'd be packing up and heading to the airport. The four dentists on the team knew the minutes were flying by, and we were all working quickly and diligently to treat as many people as possible.

Suddenly, I felt a tap on my shoulder and turned around to see my teammate and friend Paul, whose role on the team was to take care of the patients waiting in line to be treated. He had spent the entire week talking to people, hearing their stories, and sharing the love of Jesus with them. Paul and I had made many trips together over the years, and he knew what was about to happen. He told me there were still eighty-five patients standing in line, hoping to be treated, and he asked, "What am I supposed to tell them?"

Focused on managing a difficult extraction, I didn't fully engage with his question. Instead, I said, "I don't know what you're going to tell them, but we need to leave in an hour," and I went back to work. Ten minutes later, Paul tapped me on the shoulder again, and this time, his eyes were filled with tears.

"Charlie," he said, "I really need to know. What am I supposed to tell them?"

The best response I could muster was that hopefully we would be back next year, or maybe another short-term dental team would come, but I knew those were both lousy answers. Those eighty-five people would not see a dentist this year—if ever.

Paul knew that most of the people waiting in line had been suffering for years with intense tooth pain. Some had walked for as many as two days in the hopes of getting some relief. He had spoken to moms who listened in agony to their children crying themselves to sleep at night due to tooth pain, and there wasn't a thing they could do for them. He felt the desperation that gripped those eighty-five people, and he couldn't bring himself to tell them, in the face of their agony, "Maybe we will see you next year." With his tears he was saying, "Surely, we can do better than that!"

His tears pierced through my professional detachment, and for the first time I understood what this community was going through and what they would be left with when we closed up shop, left for the airport, and flew home to America.

A horrible sinking feeling struck deep in my belly as I realized I was part of the reason for Paul's tears and those of the eighty-five people in line who would soon watch us drive away. I realized I now had a new burden—one for which I could find no immediate solution.

Something Had to Change

Over the next few months, I made a decision. I was absolutely convinced that what we were doing was not the way God would do things and that he must have a better way to address the worldwide dental health problem. Jamaica is a fairly well-developed country, and yet the dental needs there are enormous. What about the rest of the far-less-developed world? The problem screamed for a new solution.

That's it, I said to myself. *I'm done. I can't do dentistry this way anymore.*

We had done good work—and it was much better than doing nothing—but I couldn't face another line of hurting, disappointed people again. I succumbed to the heartrending realization that my best efforts had fallen far short of what God intended for these communities.

"This *can't* be God's way," I said, "that we would come for a week and then nonchalantly walk away, leaving people untreated and in pain. That we would wave goodbye and say, 'Maybe we'll see you next year'? *No.* I will never do that again. *Never.*"

Then, as God would have it, I was introduced to Steve Saint, son of the famous missionary and martyr Nate Saint. I told him how torn up I was. I told him about Paul's tears and the eighty-five people we had left standing in line in Jamaica.

After listening in silence, Steve said, "Charlie, why do you treat all these patients yourself? Why don't you instead train local people in the churches to take care of the dental needs in their own communities?"

I was shocked and horrified. Surely I hadn't heard him correctly. In my mind I said, *Are you crazy? It took me four years of intense study in dental school to learn how to do this—and you're suggesting I can teach a bunch of local guys to do what I do in six days during a short-term missions trip?*

I gave Steve a noncommittal response, but I kept pondering this crazy new idea of teaching others. I thought back to my years in dental school, and how I had learned the hands-on skills I used every day as a dentist. When it was time to learn how to give a shot, the students would pair up, and we'd give each other injections. When it was time to learn how to extract a tooth, a student who was one year ahead of us taught us how to do it—and we got better the more we did it. In order to extract a tooth safely, it isn't necessary to know the embryonic origin of dental pulp or the molecular structure of lidocaine.

Gradually, it began to make sense that if my colleagues and I had been able to learn through one-on-one instruction, maybe I could pass along the essential skills in the same way. True, there will always be a need for highly skilled professionals, but there are many skills that can be delegated if we are willing to think beyond the confines of traditional Western health care and the institutions established in the Global North. The stark reality is that people were dying and suffering needlessly, with no access to dental care. Love compelled us to come up with another safe solution to address the enormous need in areas where there is no access to professional dental care. And that solution resides in the local church. The amount of suffering I had seen on previous trips demanded a response—one that would require real innovation and some calculated risk-taking.

I decided to give it a try.

Piloting a New Paradigm

I called a missionary friend in northern Ghana and asked about the dental needs in his area. He said the situation was critical—that there was only one part-time government dentist to serve three million people in that region of West Africa. My friend invited me to come with a fellow dentist to work through the local churches and train four Christian leaders in his community. We would teach them how to administer a local anesthetic and remove abscessed teeth, and we brought with us all the necessary equipment and instruments—the same high-quality tools that dentists routinely use in the US.

I remember walking into the chapel where the training would be held and seeing a very basic setup. They had brought in chairs and instruments and arranged them neatly in the front of the room. I looked at the four guys who were standing there waiting for the training to begin. They had no clue what they were getting into. Over the next six days, they would be doing things they had never imagined.

Oh, Lord, what have I agreed to? I thought. *Seriously, do you want me to train these guys to work in other people's mouths?*

Fear overwhelmed me. *Did I hear you correctly, Lord?*

I decided that if the training didn't go well, I would just pack up all the brand new donated equipment and take it back with me to the States.

Without fear, there is no courage. So we got to work.

Over the next six days, we taught those four men how to identify teeth that needed to be extracted, and they learned how to extract teeth safely and gently in closely supervised training. Then we went to a nearby village to put those new skills and knowledge into practice.

As usual, many patients were waiting for our arrival, but my colleague and I were there as trained dentists only to coach and encourage our students. Although we'd had to drop one of the students from the training program, the remaining three students each pulled more teeth in six days than I had taken out in four years of dental school.

After six days of watching these men work, we gave them the following instructions:

1. Don't start to remove a tooth unless you're confident you can finish the task.
2. Don't remove wisdom teeth; they require more advanced skills.
3. Don't leave root tips; they can become a source of infection.
4. The skill and care that you demonstrate to your patients is a reflection on you, the ministry, the church you represent, and our Lord Jesus.

Though these new dental workers could not be formally recognized as professional dentists, the training had prepared them well to identify teeth in need of treatment and perform basic extractions.

We boarded the plane to fly home, confident in their ability to treat 95 percent of the problems they would face, and praying they would have the wisdom to defer the other 5 percent. We promised to return in a year, and in the meantime we would receive regular reports. Our trainees were reminded and assured that help was just a phone call away.

Over the next year, our excitement to return to Ghana kept building; and when we got back, we were amazed at the proficiency of our trainees. Among the three of them, they had consistently been seeing sixty to eighty patients per day, three days a week, and with that amount of practice, their skill and confidence had increased dramatically.

The Impact of Compassion

My new dental colleagues had also come to realize that when patients agree to lie down in a dental chair, they are expressing vulnerability and trust. And if they trust you with their physical care, they will also trust you to talk to them about spiritual things. Jesus repeatedly used the power of physical healing to demonstrate his love for people. As health-care providers, we have the opportunity to meet people in their greatest hour of need.

We discovered that compassion, gentleness, and empathy were key values that had a great impact in teaching our new colleagues. In many cultures, schoolteachers and other trainers are harsh with their students—if they answer incorrectly they are punished. Knowing that we represented Christ, we tried to model how he taught his disciples. When they messed up, he didn't yell at them or punish them. Many people who have received our dental training have commented with amazement, "I was treated differently than I've ever been treated before." This kindness not only affects the trainees, but it also gives them a model for how to treat their patients, many of whom have never experienced that level of compassion or even heard about Jesus. Because these local health-care providers showed them the love of God in action, many who had come only to receive dental care also received Jesus into their lives.

During the first year after the initial training, the Ghanaian ministry of health made a visit to the clinic. Before their arrival, they surveyed the community to get feedback on the care received at the new dental clinic. Both the clinic and the practitioners received glowing reviews from the community. In fact, the mayor of a large nearby town, along with his gun-toting entourage, raved about the treatment they had received at the clinic. The ministry of health inspected the facilities, took note of the sterilization procedures, and were impressed by the quality of instruments being used. Satisfied, they encouraged the team to keep up the good work.

Since that time, I haven't treated patients on any missions trips; I only train nationals to do the work now. And because leaders like those in Ghana have learned how to do basic dentistry, they are viewed with the same respect as doctors, and their communities treat them with great honor. Even in heavily Muslim or Hindu cultures, these Christian leaders who have been taught to extract teeth have a high standing in their communities. They are highly valued as ones with excellent skills.

Even though at first I was shocked and appalled when Steve Saint challenged me to teach local leaders how to do dentistry, I finally realized that it is far better to pass along our skills to others and let them do the work among their own people than to pop in for a week at a time and do the work ourselves. Equipping and empowering others, rather than building dependence, gives local believers the practical skills to be the (healing) hands of Jesus to their community.

Ethical and Legal Concerns

The legality of training nonprofessionals to provide basic dental care varies by country. This concern cannot be ignored, and the in-country ministry partners must determine how they will address this challenge with their ministries of health. The incoming training team must place a huge level of trust in their local partners, to be assured that all the legal and ethical issues have been covered in advance. The last thing a team from the West wants is to bring in resources only to find out that the receiving partner isn't able to use them because the legal issues were not addressed before the training started. Generally our local church partners will take the lead, though in some countries that may not be possible.

Taking a calculated risk is one thing, but to be cavalier with the health of another human being would be both cruel and unacceptable. The results of our initial training seemed safe and effective, and the patients expressed gratitude. Follow-up with patients indicated that their dental health had improved after treatment by these dental health workers, and in many cases the improvement was profound. This model of training has been duplicated, with similar success, in at least ten frontier locations. We've heard positive stories about the impact of this model, but our commitment to following a best-practices approach requires that we should test the safety and efficacy of our training through a well-constructed, double-blind study.

Impact Assessment

In 2012, a double-blind study was conducted to compare surgical outcomes and patient satisfaction after receiving dental care from two groups of health providers. One group was composed of four indigenous dental health workers, and the other group was two American dentists. The study produced the following results:

- On average, it took the four local dental health workers twice as long to perform an extraction when compared to the American dentists. Because it took the dental health workers longer to do an extraction, there was a higher incidence of alveolar osteitis ("dry socket"), a painful postoperative condition in which a protective blood clot doesn't form properly, dislodges, or dissolves too soon, leaving the bone and nerve endings exposed. Dry socket creates more initial post-op discomfort, but it is self-limiting and heals with time.
- The level of patient satisfaction was the same between the two groups. This indicates there was no perceived difference by the patients in the quality of care received or how they felt they had been treated.
- There was no statistical difference in surgical outcomes of the two groups. Two evaluators, who were not aware of which group of caregivers treated which patients, followed up at one-, three-, and six-day intervals post-op to evaluate the physical healing of the surgery sites. Each group treated 150 patients. Although a larger sample would be better in future studies, it's very clear that the program was successful.

Because the training method works so well, the impact of my professional life has increased dramatically. The long-term influence we can have by passing along our skills to others is far greater than what we can accomplish by doing the work ourselves on short-term missions trips.

That's the story of my evolution, and I'm not alone. There are now more than fifty other dentists who are doing this kind of dental training around the world. In fact, because most countries have at least a remnant of a local church presence, I can contribute to building God's Kingdom through his church in far-off places as a dentist/trainer, without having to go as a full-time missionary.

Trained local dental health workers can treat thousands of patients per year in remote frontier regions that have little or no access to dental care. Their patients are receiving help *and* hearing the gospel, and churches are being planted as a result.

I'm no longer looked on as a hero—far from it. Now Christ and his church are being glorified because I've passed along my skills to faithful men and women who can do the work among their own people. That is truly "teaching a man to fish," and it has come about through well-planned, servant-focused, short-term missions trips with trusted partners.

Questions for Reflection and Journaling

1. What do you think of Charlie's story? Can you remember a time when you felt powerless to help people in great need and didn't know what to do?

2. We all came into this world with nothing, and we'll leave with nothing. Everything we have we received from the Lord. What gifts has God given you that he wants you to share?

3. What other skills do you have that you could teach others, with humility, knowing that it might help solve problems in a poor or underserved community?

3

FLORENCE AND THE MISSIONARIES

You never change things by fighting the existing reality. To change something, build a new model that makes the existing model obsolete.
R. BUCKMINSTER FULLER

Go therefore and make disciples of all nations, baptizing them in the name of the Father and of the Son and of the Holy Spirit, teaching them to observe all that I have commanded you.
MATTHEW 28:19-20

FLORENCE

I was born in East Africa, and my family lived in a rural Kenyan village. I remember when a mission station was built not far from our home, on the road leading toward Makueni. It was a fenced-in facility that was built, managed, and occupied by foreign missionaries. In this case, they came from England, the colonizing country that had authority over British East Africa. This mission station was primarily focused on helping the region's medical, educational, and spiritual needs.

The initial structure in the mission station was a church. A British missionary arrived and set about replacing our stick-and-mud church building with one built of concrete. During construction, he hosted short-term missions teams from his home church to help build it. The pastor was a good minister, and he tried to fit into the community.

On occasion he allowed his children to come out to play with us, and he learned the local language well enough to communicate with the villagers. On special days, he would come to our elementary school to give a devotional. He tried to build relationships with the prominent leaders in the community by visiting them for tea. Others from the community were welcome in his home, but they seldom visited the missionary unless they had a special need for financial support or medical help.

The same mission agency also sent a single, middle-aged woman to serve as the principal for a girls' boarding high school in our district. She supervised the construction of the school facility, established the management system for the school, and was the main teacher.

She was well trained, and it was a good school. Both of my older sisters went to that school. I remember that the principal had a red bicycle, and I often saw her riding to the shops and post office. She came to the church on Sundays, accompanied by her residential students.

The missionaries also built a well-equipped hospital, staffed by a doctor, nurses, and even a dentist—all funded by the British missionary agency. The hospital was well-managed, had good supplies, and was respected throughout the region for the services it provided, especially compared to the government health facilities. It was known as the place to go for good medical care. When I was growing up, that's where my family would go for treatment. It had a very good reputation, and the missionaries from the United Kingdom who ran the hospital were looked up to and honored by the community.

The End of an Era

We were surprised when the pastor and his family suddenly left Africa to return to England so their children could attend a British secondary school. We were further surprised when the British mission agency didn't send a replacement. The pastor hadn't mentored or trained anyone to replace himself, so even though we continued to meet, our local congregation struggled. A local pastor finally stepped up to take over the work, and the missionary house was ultimately converted into a secular guesthouse. Over time, the congregation began to grow under the local leadership, and the community eventually constructed a larger brick church building to accommodate more people.

Sadly, not long after the pastor's departure, the principal of the mission boarding school died in a horrible traffic accident. She also hadn't mentored any local teachers, and without trained leadership the school experienced several financial setbacks. It was eventually taken over by the government, which of course began to operate it not as a Christian school but as a government school. Though the education continued, it no longer had a spiritual aspect.

Then the government built a hospital in the nearby town of Wote. As the new facility grew in quality and reputation, the public's use of the mission hospital declined. Soon the old missionary hospital was downgraded to a health clinic, run by a secular Kenyan nurse, and no longer had any connection to a church or ministry. In the span of a single generation, all three cross-cultural missionary activities—the church, the school, and the hospital—drifted away from their original vision.

An interesting thing to observe is how the three parts of the mission were disconnected from each other. The hospital, school, and church were all independent, vertical activities related to the mission, but there was no real interaction. The only resource they shared in common was location—having all been built on the mission station by the same agency. But they didn't help each other by taking up the slack and filling in the gaps when one ministry or another had a need. Instead of the stronger parts lifting up the weaker as one part struggled or failed, it dragged the others down with it. And none of the entities had a succession plan or an exit strategy.

God gave me the opportunity as I was growing up to experience this missions model firsthand, and I am so thankful for that eye-opening experience. It helped me see that the mission station near my home was able to do good work for a short time, but their efforts did not endure and did not produce real transformation. There was no transfer of skills from the missionaries to the local community, and no training or mentoring of local leaders. In retrospect, it seems they didn't see that as part of their mission.

Sadly, the message they inadvertently communicated was that the local population probably wasn't capable of doing the work themselves; in other words, that foreign missionaries had come to help, and they alone would build and manage the work for the local community.

The "Top Down" Model of Missions

Along with the rest of the people living in that region, my family looked up to the expatriate missionaries. They were the providers, which made us the receivers; and because of that relationship, we became dependent on them. As the providers of quality health care, good education, and strong faith, they were seen as heroes. They had the authority and the expertise, and the local population was never mentored, trained, or included in leadership.

For anyone who has lived, as I have, in a colony ruled by a foreign power,[†] the loss of self-government will always set off internal alarms. Colonizers arrive with power. They take authority and jurisdiction. As the ruling power, they expect to be respected. Often they are feared, and seldom are they truly liked or trusted. If you grew up under a colonial system, that mentality stays with you, and it carries over to all foreign authority figures, including foreign missionaries.

But even though this paternalistic, or colonial, model of missions had its problems, it became a vital part of the local community; and when this model disintegrated, it created a vacuum. When the missionaries left, the services went with them, along with the work of ministry, and the local communities were left wondering what to do next. This traditional style of missions was the common practice for decades.

[†] Kenya was a British colony from 1920 to 1963.

Although I grew up witnessing an outdated missions model, that's not to say there were no good results. I came to know Christ through those missionaries, my sisters went to the mission school, and many people—including members of my own family—were cared for in the mission hospital.

For a long time, I thought this was the only way that missions was done. But at age thirteen, I left my village to attend a boarding high school in the city, and there I was exposed to other models of ministry and missionary work.

Searching for a New Model

After I graduated from high school, I sensed a call to become a missionary—but I knew I wanted to do it differently than what I had seen growing up. I didn't want to stand out as the hero. I wanted to work with the poor and serve them humbly, while involving them in the process of their own long-term development. And I wanted to show them Christ and his love.

Though I had grown up in a Protestant church and had gone to a school with Protestant influence, I decided I wanted to become a Catholic missionary. Their missionary style seemed closest to the picture I had in mind. Their practice of giving themselves fully to their ministry seemed more like an act of worship than a job. It looked more like a commitment than simply doing a task. The Catholic nuns offered their lives, not just their service. They made vows of lifelong commitment, not only for as long as family arrangements made their service convenient. They practiced their faith daily and took prayer seriously.

When I saw Catholic nuns serving people, especially in hospitals or among the poor, I noticed how they related closely to the people. They connected intimately with the destitute, and they demonstrated Christ's love and compassion. That was the model I wanted to emulate.

I told the significant people in my life about my plans to become a Catholic nun and move into a convent. My pastor told me that I could practice the Catholic style of service that I admired without actually converting to Catholicism. My family, especially my big sister, strongly advised me to get married and raise a family. My boyfriend, Festus, who was preparing to propose marriage, assured me it would be much more fulfilling if we served together as a couple and raised our children on the mission field. I recognized this as good counsel, and I took it to heart.

I finally came to realize that it's not so much about whether you take vows as a nun or enter another vocation; it's about living like Christ. It's the status of your heart that defines you, rather than a religious order or a title. I realized that I could be married, become a medical doctor, and serve God with all the dedication and commitment I admired in the nuns—and I could do it as a Protestant missionary.

Finding a New Way

The old way of doing missions has a lot of history to overcome. It is not an easy model to change, because it gives the service providers some major advantages. It gives them ownership and control.

But the world around us is changing. Indigenous missions agencies are springing up. Missionaries from non-Western cultures are going out in increasing numbers around the world. Churches have been planted in unbelievably difficult areas. For the most part, even in closed countries, Christians from that culture who speak the local language as well as English can be identified, equipped, and mobilized to speed up the work. The advantages of working cooperatively within the culture are numerous, beyond the obvious cost savings.

The search for a new way of doing missions takes us back to Jesus' way of ministry: He turned his disciples into coworkers in just three years. Even though they were far from perfect, they were hands-on participants. Jesus modeled ministry for them, delegated to them, and invested in them the authority to accomplish their mission.

Jesus instructed Peter to feed his sheep—even with the knowledge that Peter had denied him. That would seem to border on recklessness. He even sent his disciples out to minister on their own, without him. Then he handed over his ministry to them entirely. He phased out his hands-on role after completing a pilot program in his local area, telling his disciples, "Go and make disciples of all nations."

Jesus multiplied himself in those he served. He came not just to give service. His role was to demonstrate, train, empower, and step back to facilitate the establishment of his Father's Kingdom on earth, leaving it in the hands of the people his Father chose.

As his disciples, we are to follow the same path.

Questions for Reflection and Journaling

1. Thinking back on your own childhood, how did you observe people helping others? Was it done well? In what ways could their efforts have been improved?

2. How do you think those early examples influenced your approach to ministry today?

3. Who is the best role model for the kind of image-bearer of Christ you aspire to emulate in your life and ministry?

4. What was eye-opening for you about Florence's story, seeing Western missionaries through the perspective of a Kenyan village girl? What could the Western missionaries have done differently to involve the community?

UNITED IN PRAYER IN KABUL

There is a tremendous strength that is growing in the world through sharing together, praying together, suffering together, and working together.
MOTHER TERESA

When he saw the crowds, he had compassion for them, because they were harassed and helpless, like sheep without a shepherd.
MATTHEW 9:36

CHARLIE

We arrived in Afghanistan right after the Taliban had been officially overthrown. That shift in power ended an Islamic theocracy that had eviscerated the Afghans' civil and political rights—especially for women. The Taliban had prohibited girls from attending secondary school and prevented women across the country from working outside their homes.[1] Human rights violations were rampant. The country's economic situation was dire with widespread poverty and food insecurity.[2]

As the Taliban was driven out in December 2001, the door was nudged open for Christian ministry in Afghanistan. Southeast Christian Church was ready for this opportunity. Preparations had been made for a medical missions trip, including setting up a clinic and a guesthouse, but it was an intimidating prospect. I was invited on this medical mission as a dentist, and Florence was invited as a doctor and missions partner of the church.

"Will you join us to discern God's will?" the church leaders asked each of us. "We want you to pray and listen, and then to speak into the resulting plans."

We were a small team flying into Kabul—only eight people—but the medical screening we planned would provide an entry into the culture to assess health needs, triage and examine patients, and provide a diagnosis for the community. Florence already had been doing similar health screenings in Ethiopia and knew the value of presenting real data to community leaders.

Working in a Hostile Environment

This was not your usual missions trip. Every member of the team knew it was extremely risky to be in Afghanistan so soon after the Taliban had fallen.[3] We were told we might encounter land mines. That will get your attention! We knew there were big problems in Afghanistan. Although the Taliban was out of power, they weren't really gone; you just couldn't tell who was who. The ever-present threat of renewed violence enveloped the country.

Christians still could not worship openly. Beatings, torture, and kidnappings were common for Afghan believers. Many Christians were martyred, and their deaths generally occurred without public knowledge. Some new believers had been imprisoned, but more often Christian converts from Islam were killed by their own family members before any legal proceedings could begin.[4]

Both local and national governments in Afghanistan have a history of being openly opposed to Christianity, and 99.8 percent of the population is Muslim.[5]

Knowing all this, our small missions team felt understandably nervous and vulnerable. Within two days of our arrival at a small village north of Kabul, we realized that the villagers' physical, emotional, and social needs were just as dire as their spiritual needs. We were overwhelmed by what we saw, and we knew we were way out of our element working in these difficult circumstances. The women were fully covered in their burkas, and they would allow us to work on their teeth only after all the Afghan men had left the room. A few of the women were willing to expose their entire face to give us better access to their teeth, but most would raise the face covering just enough for us to do our work. The willingness of these women to be treated by foreign men indicates the level of pain they were in and the desperation they felt. Especially in Afghanistan, women's overall health was much worse than the men's. Women's health was not a priority.[6]

As we continued our medical work, we quickly began filling all our spare time with prayer.

That prayer time was like a magnet. It drew all members of the team together, with each other and with the Lord. We all were mature believers and skilled professionals, familiar with international ministry, but even with all our years of preparation, we knew we needed God's leading and his hand of protection more than anything else. So we committed ourselves to gather early every morning on the mountain overlooking the remote village to pray before doing any work.

Prayer Was Our Priority

The old hotel where we set up our clinic had been hit by a five-hundred-pound bomb, and everyone in the village carried AK-47s, even the eight-year-old boys. Everywhere you turned, there was evidence of death and destruction. We realized that the only hope for Afghanistan was for God to intervene. There was nothing we could do but pray. So that's what we did. Above all else, we felt compelled to pray.

Those early morning prayer times not only calmed our fears, but they also became the most important and most memorable moments of the trip. That was when we united to ask God for his leading and guidance for every step we would take and every decision we would make that day. We prayed for each other and for our families back home, as well as for the Afghan people—both the secret Christians who had to worship in hiding, as well as the vast majority of Afghan people who had never met a Christian and had no idea what good news the gospel message offered them.

I remember being captivated when I heard Florence pray for the overwhelmingly enormous physical and spiritual needs in that country. She prayed for hope to become evident. This was my first time meeting Florence. I had heard of her and of the Life In Abundance ministry because of my involvement with SECC missions, and I found myself drawn to the spiritual depth of this soft-spoken woman from East Africa.

Although there was no visible Christian church in Afghanistan, we had heard there were secret believers who were understandably afraid to identify themselves. More than anything, we could sense the spiritual warfare all around us, and we prayed for God's hedge of protection against it.

When I reflect on those early morning prayer times, I recall how prayer bonded us together as a team and gave us a deep passion for the Afghan people, their country, and the work we had come to do. Those prayer times were the sure and solid foundation on which God built that medical mission to Kabul.

Instead of focusing on the fear, risk, danger, and oppression in Afghanistan, we began to catch a glimpse of God's love and compassion for this land. We began to see hope in the eyes of the people we served, and together we came up with new ideas for how to best help them.

In prayer, Florence recognized the need to bring in more help to gather health data, like the people she had trained to do health screenings in Ethiopia and Kenya. She put out the word, and a young woman I will refer to as Claire, who had interned with LIA in Kenya, volunteered to come and help with the work. When the findings were presented to the village elders, they said, "No one has ever come to help us the way you have."

Our work had a lasting impact on both the village and the team members. As a result of the time there, Claire and her husband felt called into full-time vocational Christian service. They later moved to the nation with the largest Muslim population in the world, Indonesia, where they still serve today.

At the conclusion of the trip, Florence returned to Kenya, and I flew home to Kentucky, determined to make prayer an even greater part of my ministry. The practice of prayer was already a strong part of the culture at Life In Abundance, where they commit themselves every Monday to a special day of prayer and fasting by the entire staff.

A few years later, when I became missions director at Southeast Christian Church, I began a daily morning time of prayer with the missions team that became an inspiration to the church staff. Corporate team prayer is the best team-building exercise there is.

It was in Afghanistan that I fully realized the power of prayer to unify a team and the importance of ministering to one another in that way. Those times of early morning prayer also cemented my friendship with Florence. We built a cooperative relationship that has propelled us to travel across the globe to evaluate needs, seek God's heart, and minister to refugees (e.g., in nations such as Poland, Jamaica, Ghana, and Italy).

The beauty and power of what occurred during our daily morning prayer times was a wake-up call to realize that we *cannot*—and *must not*—attempt to do missions in our own strength and wisdom. We need God's presence and his leading 100 percent of the time and 100 percent of the way.

The Afghanistan trip also solidified the relationship between Life In Abundance and Southeast Christian Church. As we approached God in like-minded fashion, he answered our prayers. Since that time, untold numbers of Afghans have come to faith in Christ, and the underground house church movement is growing. Florence and I have both been changed as well.

Florence says she will never go anywhere for ministry unless she knows that it has first been bathed in prayer. She has made it a priority for her staff to pray for one country per week. Every Sunday evening, she personally puts together the prayer list for each country where LIA serves and sends it to each global office. The fact that it comes from the founder and president of the organization communicates to the entire staff the importance that Florence places on it. Their prayer time has unified the staff and given them all a Kingdom perspective on their work.

For me personally, the experience of praying together early each morning in Kabul showed me how much there is to learn from others in corporate prayer. And I learned that the time spent with others in prayer is certainly not wasted time—in fact, it just might be the most important "work" we do in a day.

Questions for Reflection and Journaling

1. How important is prayer in your life right now?

2. Describe a time when you felt powerless without God's help.

3. What is God speaking to you about regarding the priority prayer can have in your current schedule?

4. How do you intend to make more time for effectual prayer in your daily routine?

5

OVERWHELMED ON CHRISTMAS EVE IN ETHIOPIA

In a world where everything revolves around yourself—protect yourself, promote yourself, comfort yourself, and take care of yourself— Jesus says, "Crucify yourself. Put aside all self-preservation in order to live for God's glorification, no matter what that means for you in the culture around you."

DAVID PLATT

I have been crucified with Christ. It is no longer I who live, but Christ who lives in me.

GALATIANS 2:20

FLORENCE

My heart was broken with a zeal to change the plight of the poor and the vulnerable. The pursuit of a clear call led us to Ethiopia more than two decades ago. My husband, Festus, went to lead the national team for our missions agency, and I went as his wife—and also as a medical doctor. I soon started a community-based medical ministry for the more than five thousand people living in the leprosy-affected slum community surrounding the All Africa Leprosy, Tuberculosis, and Rehabilitation Training Centre in the capital city of Addis Ababa. As our new ministry began to grow and thrive, to say I was busy would be a huge understatement: I was a doctor, wife, ministry leader, and mother of two small boys.

We were nearing the Christmas holidays, and I felt a deep sadness for the children of the families we were serving. I knew they would have no celebration at all—no gifts, no excitement, no special meal, nothing different from any other day. I really wanted to do something nice for these children so they could experience the joy of Christmas.

I decided to host a one-day Christmas Eve Vacation Bible School (VBS). I posted an announcement, inviting children to register to attend.

The next morning the children started coming very, very early and made so much noise in their excitement that we couldn't sleep. By the time I made my way out to the gate of the missions complex, the watchmen had been registering children for hours, taking their names and giving them numbers. I was astonished to find there were already four hundred names on the list! I never expected anything close to that many, and I could see more children still coming.

I quickly asked the watchmen to stop giving out numbers, and I put up a notice that registration was closed and we couldn't handle any more children. In fact, I had no idea how we'd handle the many who had already signed up.

I had been thinking this would be a simple party, with tea and bread and some stories from the Bible; but for these children, it would be the highlight of their Christmas holiday. I could hear the sounds of disappointment from those who arrived at our door too late to sign up. But the realization that four hundred poor children would be at my home the very next day was already starting to overwhelm me, and I am not easily overwhelmed.

I didn't know what to do, so I contacted the small local church and humbly asked if they could possibly arrange some volunteers to help me. They agreed to see what could be done at this late hour.

Then, very early the next morning, I drove into the city to buy supplies for the party.

It was Christmas Eve, and I knew the demand for bread would be high. I needed to get to the bakeries before they sold out. I arrived early, but supplies were already low, and I had to go to many shops to obtain enough bread for the hungry kids who would be our Christmas guests.

After several other stops, my shopping was finally done.

It was still very early, and this Christmas Eve morning had dawned wet and cold. Mist hung low over the road as I was driving home, with my car full of delightfully fragrant bread. The weather and the early hour meant there wasn't much traffic, which helped me feel less stressed and allowed me to relax and get more into the Christmas spirit.

Suddenly, a dark shape appeared in the road ahead of me. I braked quickly to avoid hitting it.

Coming to a full stop, I peered through the mist at this slowly moving form, still unsure what it was. Then it moved again, and a head appeared and faced me. It was a woman, and on her back was a tiny baby. I saw the woman's deformed nose and hands and immediately recognized the debilitating effects of leprosy. Her feet and legs were also crippled and maimed by the disease, and although she was moving as quickly as she could to safely cross the road with her child, it was barely the speed of a crawl.

There was nothing I could do at that moment to help her, so I kept my car stopped in the middle of the road, preventing any other car from passing, so she would be in less danger of getting hit.

As I watched her ever-so-slowly cross the road, I realized she had come from the trash pit on the outskirts of my community. My focus shifted to the huge smoldering pile of rubbish. Clambering over the steaming garbage was a large group of young children—five, six, seven years old, and some maybe younger—picking quickly through the trash, anxiously looking for a partially eaten meal, a half-rotted piece of fruit, or some chicken bones . . . anything to eat.

Just as I knew I needed to arrive early at the bakery, this woman with her tiny baby knew she had to get to the trash pit early if she was to have any chance of scavenging a meal.

My heart was broken. I had no idea this was happening so close to my home.

The children looked up from their foraging and noticed I had stopped the car. En masse, they ran from the trash pit and rushed to my car window to beg. Being from Nairobi, home to the two largest slums in Africa, I was no stranger to street children and beggars. But as these kids pressed up against my car, with their pleading faces and tiny hands gesturing to their mouths, their eyes locked with mine, and I immediately realized the depth of their misery, anxiety, and fear. I understood their desperation to find some food or a few coins, otherwise they might not get anything to eat that day. I saw how they were looking at me with a mixture of fear, despair, and hope—as they smelled the delicious aroma of a carload of fresh bread.

Fighting to control my emotions, I thought, *This just isn't right! It can't be—especially not at Christmas!*

My maternal instincts almost overwhelmed my sensibilities—I came very close to telling these children to follow me home and I would find a space for them to live with my family. Then I considered giving them the bread I had just bought. But if I did, what would I serve the four hundred children who would soon be arriving expectantly in my backyard? I thought that perhaps I could start an orphanage—there obviously was a great need for something meaningful to be done for these kids. I wanted to take some immediate, positive, life-changing action—but what? How could I sit here and witness this horrific sight and then just drive away to finish my preparations for Christmas?

But that's what I did.

I drove back to the house, prepared for the VBS with the help of the volunteers from the local church, and welcomed the hundreds of excited children. I shared with them the wonderful story of the birth of Jesus, God's Son, who came to redeem us from the sin and injustice in this world and give us abundant life. The party was a fun and memorable time for everyone.

Still, the image of the woman with leprosy, with her baby on her back, and the faces of the kids from the trash pit stayed in the forefront of my mind, haunting me for days. Something had to be done, and I agonized over the problem, trying to come up with a solution, a program—something—to help fix this horribly broken situation.

Finally, I came to the sober realization that I couldn't fix it. It wasn't going to be solved by my giving out bread. It wasn't going to be solved by my starting an orphanage. Even my important work of treating their medical needs and creating a healthier community wouldn't be the cure. Nothing I did, or could ever do, would be enough to fix even this one problem in one small community on the outskirts of one city in Ethiopia.

I was limited, and the problem seemed insurmountably limitless.

But what I *could* do was pray, and I began praying intensely for this situation. I had no doubts about my calling, but I questioned my methods and effectiveness. I knew that Father God sees things better than I do, and he must have a solution. So I went to him repeatedly, asking what his desire was for those children and what I might do to help them.

After a long season of prayer, as I continued searching for answers, God brought my mind back to that Christmas Eve VBS party. I had initiated a well-intentioned program on a whim, and quickly became aware that I was in way over my head. I was overwhelmed and anxious. I knew I was incapable of serving, entertaining, and teaching four hundred children, while keeping them corralled and helping them behave. It was an impossible task for any one person—just as the great need I witnessed at the trash pit was too much for any one individual to solve.

In humility, I realized that the only reason the Christmas Eve party had been successful was that wonderful people from the local church had volunteered to help me. They came and worked tirelessly, and somehow everything came together. They saved the day. Without them, I have no doubt the entire event would have been a massive failure.

As I began to thank God for those kind people and their willingness to serve, he helped me realize that the local church was the instrument he wanted to use to change communities. God's long-term solution for the trash pits of the world is not a massive influx of expat missionaries coming in with all the answers and resources;

instead, it is the local indigenous church actively living out the love of Christ among their neighbors.

I realized that my assignment was to help the local church grasp the importance of their role in the community, to equip and empower them to be able to accomplish that vital role successfully, and to help them identify the local resources and assets they could employ to enable the work to be self-sustainable over the long term. The missionaries would be the helpers, the trainers, the behind-the-scenes people who would be there for a limited time to build up and lift up the local body of Christ to accomplish the work of redemption and reconciliation. I did not want to follow in the footsteps of the traditional missionaries I had observed growing up. It was time to forge a new path and connect with the poor, the sick, and the disadvantaged in a different way.

A New Vision

We would still go into their communities, but not to build a long-term ministry for ourselves; we would be invited in as trusted partners of the local church to advise, train, help, and encourage. And then—at a predetermined point in time, without any fanfare—we would leave. The local church would carry on the work. The church would be the heroes in the community, and Christ would receive the glory.

That became the genesis of the model that is a guiding principle for Life In Abundance to this day: We work alongside the local church and keep it at the very center of all that we do. We are not there to build our brand or increase our fame. You won't see our logo on the projects we start. We work to exalt Christ through his bride, the church, as she works to transform lives, communities, and nations.

Those few minutes in the middle of the road near the trash pit, in the very early hours of Christmas Eve, broke me. The experience sent me to my knees, and then set my feet on a new path. God in his mercy and grace helped me to see his plan for reaching the world, a model that gives glory where it is due: to the name of Jesus Christ.

Here are the essential elements of the strategy:

- It lifts up the local church to become vitally relevant in the daily life of the community.
- It makes use of the entire body of Christ, leveraging partnerships with outside organizations under the leadership of the local church.
- It decreases the vertical, non-collaborative role of outside organizations.
- It helps the vulnerable become empowered in their own communities.
- It gives dignity to "the least of these," the ones Jesus calls "my brothers and sisters."[1]
- It addresses the systemic and root causes of poverty to provide solutions for the affected.
- It enables the poor to participate in and take ownership of their own development.

This new approach is not nearly as easy as feeding people for a day, or as organized as taking charge and being seen as the hero, but it's far more effective.

If I hadn't encountered that disfigured woman and those hungry children on that Christmas Eve morning, it's very likely I would still be busy ministering in that same community, doing good medical work to the best of my ability. The people would be healthier, but they would still be looking to me as the hero—someone with the knowledge and position to improve their lives—and I would naively be taking glory for myself that rightfully belongs to God.

God doesn't call us to pursue recognition, fame, and glory for ourselves. To the contrary, he calls us to crucify the part of us that seeks to exalt ourselves. He calls us to partner with and equip the local church so that we can leave behind a greater capacity for impact in the places we have been called to serve.

As we have sought God's way of doing things, he has shown us how sustainable development can be achieved. It was his excellent plan all along. To him be all the glory.

Questions for Reflection and Journaling

1. What needs or opportunities have you or your church missed that are happening close to home? Where, or what, is your local "trash pit"?

2. How has God surprised you and led your life in new directions that you did not expect? In what circumstances have you learned to depend on God and not just on yourself?

3. Where do you sense God is leading you now, and what lessons is he teaching you through the situations you're wrestling with currently?

6

AN INVITATION
TO A DIFFERENT WAY

Think different.

CRAIG TANIMOTO

Every branch in me that does not bear fruit he takes away, and every
branch that does bear fruit he prunes, that it may bear more fruit.

JOHN 15:2

CHARLIE

I remember walking through a very poor community in Kisumu,
Kenya, with the pastor of a large American church. We were with
a missions partner, visiting some of the people the local church was
working with in their program of transformational development.
When we stepped off the main thoroughfare into an impoverished
neighborhood, the smells, sights, and sounds of this urban slum
assaulted our senses, underscoring the magnitude of the need.

We entered the tiny, rundown shack of a widow who was infected
with HIV/AIDS. Though she was receiving the latest HIV treatment
available through a local clinic, this poor, sick, single mom was struggling to tend to her own needs while also taking care of her three
young children. We learned that, through the outreach of the local

church, this woman had become a Christian and was taking part in the job training program offered by the church. She was obviously in bad health and financially poor—certainly compared to the members of the American pastor's congregation—and to all appearances her situation seemed hopeless.

Looking at the woman's surroundings, the pastor was overcome with concern and compassion. When he saw the needy kids, he immediately thought of child sponsorship as the solution. He knew he had resources that could make an immediate difference for these children, and being a man of action, he wanted to help them right now.

As he started to reach for his wallet, he said, "I'm going to take care of these kids for her." It's the same reaction most of us would have when facing such heartbreaking conditions. We see a great need and we want to fix it.

Fortunately, our local missions partner realized what the pastor was doing and stopped him from pulling out his wallet. He explained to the pastor that this young mother was part of a microfinance program, through which she had received a small loan from a table bank (a member-owned-and-operated savings and credit group) created at her local church. From the proceeds of the loan, she had started a small business, selling french fries from a table set up outside her home. With the money she received from that income-generating activity, she was able to pay back her loan and provide food for her family. So although she looked hopelessly poor to the comparatively rich American pastor, she was actually doing much better than when she had started the program, and she was on her way to becoming self-sufficient.

That kind of transformation probably never would have happened if she had been handed a wad of American dollars instead of business training and a loan. And when the dollars had all been spent, her children would be hungry again, and not enrolled in school, and the mother would probably be sitting inside her shack, waiting for the next handout from a benevolent foreigner. Instead, she had become an example to her three children, and to her community, of what can happen when alleviating poverty is approached from a wholistic perspective—where long-term transformation is the goal, and short-term fixes are rarely the solution. Ministry that reflects God's heart of compassion for the poor produces fruit that remains long-term and doesn't create dependence on outside intervention.

Where Does It Hurt?

As medical professionals, Florence and I adhere to the Hippocratic principle "to do good or to do no harm."[1] We are accustomed to asking, "Where does it hurt?" to determine the root cause of a patient's complaint. In diagnosing a medical issue, our desire is not only to take away the pain, but also to reach the real source of that pain and treat the underlying condition.

The same question—Where does it hurt?—could be asked in evaluating global missions activity. Missiologists and researchers have examined the symptoms and undertaken the difficult diagnostic work to dig deep into our systems to uncover bad practices that have resulted in widespread hurt throughout the world of missions. But as part of our global missions strategy, working together as churches and ministry organizations to alleviate world poverty, we must come to the sober realization that the pain is *systemic*—that is, it has spread throughout the entire missions structure. If we are to *do good and do no harm*, we must reevaluate our systems.

Though there has been a lot of traditional missions activity over the past century, we still haven't accomplished the task of reaching the world for Christ. Many excellent books have been written to explain why traditional missions efforts have not been more effective at eliminating poverty while seeking to make disciples in every nation. We recommend two in particular—*Toxic Charity: How Churches and Charities Hurt Those They Help (and How to Reverse It)* by Robert D. Lupton; and *When Helping Hurts: How to Alleviate Poverty without Hurting the Poor . . . and Yourself* by Steve Corbett and Brian Fikkert—to help you understand the problems that arise as we attempt to eradicate poverty and share the gospel.

Unfortunately, in the fear that they would do further harm by trying to help, far too many people overreacted and simply stopped doing anything. People and organizations with the means to do much far-reaching good recognized the unintended consequences of their actions but were unaware of proven alternative solutions or models to follow instead. Shell-shocked, they became paralyzed and inactive—for fear of doing more harm or wasting their efforts and resources—but their caution and inaction only exacerbated the problems they sought to alleviate. Donor fatigue has also become a factor, because dependency is exhausting for donors and recipients alike.

If doing good is better than doing nothing, how can we ensure that our good work does not produce harm? One way is to remember that we have a God who sees everything—and he sees it far better than we do. When evaluating systems or problems in a culture, wouldn't it make sense to inquire of God for *his* solution?

Quick Diagnosis, Quick Cure

North Americans, by and large, are results-driven and goal-oriented. Our life experience, education, and business training have taught us to survey a situation quickly, devise a strategy to fix what is broken (while ignoring a maxim I once heard that "the best solutions often come from those closest to the problem"[2]), commit resources to it, find a quick fix, celebrate the short-term success (without even realizing we have stomped on the dignity of the brothers and sisters we are seeking to help), and move on to fix something else. But the brokenness found in poverty situations is not easily fixed. Serious solutions must go far beyond simply treating the symptoms by providing short-term material aid.

In medicine, we devise a course of treatment based on our

understanding of the root causes of the problem. If we get it right and treat it properly, the patient gets better. However, if we misdiagnose, we may also mistreat, and the patient may get worse—even dangerously so. For example, if we determine that a person has a virus and therefore prescribe treatment for the flu instead of doing a blood test and discovering they have malaria, the patient could die or have serious, long-term aftereffects. That is doing real, permanent harm.

The same principle applies to poverty. If we diagnose the problem as ignorance, and the cause as a lack of knowledge, we will bring in teachers, build schools, and educate the population. If we think the problem is systemic discrimination and the cause is greed and oppression, we will work for social justice. But the underlying causes of problems in a community are not always clear. The people we are trying to help may not be able to pinpoint where it hurts. They may not know the full extent of their needs or be completely honest with themselves to admit it if they did—let alone level with rich foreigners (or well-meaning politicians) arriving to give them things. We all like quick solutions, but an accurate diagnosis—one that addresses the true underlying causes—may require a long and difficult (but ultimately beneficial) course of treatment.

No More Lone Rangers

The key to treating the problem of global poverty lies in close interaction with a trusted local partner. And we believe the church is the best change agent for community transformation.

As a dentist and a doctor, it pains us to admit that medical professionals are sometimes seen as driven, overconfident, and too often arrogant. Perhaps it's because our chosen occupations have tasked us with fixing, or at least maintaining, what God has created. Whatever the underlying reason, that pride sometimes leads to wrong diagnoses.

The same thing happens when people of means walk into an impoverished village or neighborhood. Our abilities and resources can convey an attitude of superiority and send the subtle but debilitating message that those whom we seek to help are somehow inferior and desperately needy for any crumbs we may brush from our well-stocked tables.

Dealing with Spiritual Poverty

Ending poverty is a laudable goal in itself, but the primary issue we must address is broken relationships with God. Whether people are materially rich or poor, they will always be spiritually destitute until they are made right with him. Our goal cannot be only to ensure that a community can sustainably provide its own food needs if their well-nourished bodies house starving souls. If they are physically healthy but are not enjoying the fullness of the abundant life that comes from living in harmony with God and in a way that glorifies him, then their fundamental problem has not actually been solved.

This primary transformation—rebuilding people's broken relationships with God—cannot happen without the active involvement of the local church. Only through the church will people continue to mature spiritually and learn to be change agents, making a lasting difference in their communities long after the missionaries and development ministries have left. And then they can be involved in solving their other related problems. That's why the successful model you are about to discover emerges from a vibrant, engaged local church.

The body of Christ needs every part of the entire body, and working together synergistically, we are much more powerful, much more efficient, and much more effective than going it alone. That's why it's God's plan: "There is one body and one Spirit—just as you were called to the one hope that belongs to your call—one Lord, one faith, one baptism, one God and Father of all, who is over all and through all and in all."[3] We might be on the opposite ends of the earth, but we're one family.

God has chosen and ordained the local church to be the instrument of his love and grace on earth. Parachurch organizations are doing a great job of evangelizing and providing materials, but they cannot take the place of the local church. Christian ministries also tend to come and go, but God has put a leadership structure in place through his church for ongoing sustainability.

Unfortunately, when you visit a local church in many impoverished communities, it's difficult to imagine how it could ever rise to take on such a vital task. However, the church—even in its worst state—is still the way Jesus chose to work in the world. So we need to partner with the local church, seeing it as Christ sees it, and knowing that in this process, it can become vibrant and engaged.

Helping Doesn't Need to Hurt

We know that helping can hurt, but we have also discovered that it doesn't have to. Helping can also heal.

What if we come alongside the work God has already started? What if we pray together, learn together, and apply biblical principles together? What if we see where God is working and go in that direction, joining in what he's doing?

We intend this book to be a resource of solutions for you. We'll introduce you to a different and better way of ministering to the poor—a proven model that we've seen bring about lasting transformation, both in the Global North and South. We'll also share with you the biblical principles that have come out of these stories—principles we now implement to guide healthy partnerships between Western (and other comparatively rich) donors and local indigenous organizations. And these principles can apply to any local cross-cultural community as well. If that interests you, and we pray it does, read on.

Questions for Reflection and Journaling

1. In what ways do you live as if the rest of the world doesn't exist? How could you and your church better support the poor in your area?

2. Do you have a heart of compassion for the disadvantaged? How is it affecting your decisions?

3. Are there actions that you've thought were helpful but now realize may have done harm?

4. What insights and ideas do you have about spreading God's love to people who desperately need to know him?

PART 2

PRINCIPLES OF TRANSFORMATIONAL DEVELOPMENT

7

WHAT IS TRANSFORMATIONAL DEVELOPMENT?

On the one hand, we are called to play the Good Samaritan on life's roadside; but that will be only an initial act. One day we must come to see that the whole Jericho road must be transformed so that men and women will not be constantly beaten and robbed as they make their journey on life's highway.

MARTIN LUTHER KING JR.

The Spirit of the Lord GOD is upon me, because the LORD has anointed me to bring good news to the poor.

ISAIAH 61:1

FLORENCE

I was out in the bush in rural Kenya, conducting a health education seminar for Maasai women. It was during our early years working with that population. My goal was to teach them basic hygiene and thereby improve the health of their families. The women all seemed skeptical when I talked about the value of taking a full-body bath. Based on myths and superstitions from their folklore, they believed bathing was hazardous. But one of the ladies, the pastor's wife, decided to take the risk and give it a try anyway.

After the seminar, she went home, heated up some water, found something to use for a tub—I believe it was a cattle trough—went behind her house, and took her first full bath. It was so wonderful and relaxing! She had the best night's sleep in a long time. The next morning, she gathered more wood, heated more water, and took another bath before returning to the class. She was about an hour late for the session and disturbed everyone with her excitement. When she walked in, she was literally glowing. She raved about how delightful and refreshing her first tub bath had been, saying she had slept so well that she believed she might actually be in heaven. And this morning, she said, all she wanted to do was take another bath. Shiny and clean, she was jumping up and down as she told the story, almost giggling about how young she felt. And that one personal testimony kick-started the practice of bathing in the community.

This woman had been transformed by a single bath. Her belief system had changed, and she became an advocate for cleanliness in this dusty, remote, nomadic setting. That incident reminded me of how many good things we miss when we believe the lies we've been told. We settle for less and even come to believe there's no other way of doing things than how we've always done them.

This Maasai woman experienced a change in mindset, and it affected everyone around her. She now had joy, along with improved hygiene, better sleep, and a realization that the old superstitions might not be true after all.

Creating Significant Change

When most nongovernmental organizations (NGOs) or ministries talk about the work of *development*, they are referring to the process of change in a person's life and community. Typically they work toward changing people's economic or material status—helping them move from being monetarily poor to being able to provide adequate housing, food, and education for themselves and their dependents.

While this level of development is obviously a good step in the right direction, we prefer to work for *transformational development*. It's not simply a different term; it's a completely different concept—opening eyes and minds to significant change that affects the entire person.

As we sought God's wisdom and leading, and diligently searched the Scriptures, we found several biblical principles that form the foundation for how we approach transformational development. In the next twelve chapters, we will examine several of these key biblical principles—all of which are necessary to bring lasting change to a community:

- centering everything in prayer
- maintaining an eternal perspective
- loving the whole person
- using relief and development wisely
- fostering healthy short-term missions teams
- giving glory to God and his church
- partnering in unity with the local church
- making disciples
- developing a biblical strategy

We have found that grasping these biblical principles and internalizing them as part of our daily lives makes it possible to bring about lasting change and real transformation in the communities we serve.

This is more than just working to bring economic development or spiritual awakening to the poor—as if the coin of poverty had only two sides: monetary wealth and spiritual health. *Transformation* speaks of wide-ranging, wholistic,[†] and systemic change that affects every part of a person or community.

Pursuing Wholistic Transformational Development

When we are invited into a community, we look deeper than the obvious indicators of economic poverty. We also engage with the many areas of injustice—confronting enslaving powers to bring freedom, redemption, and a future to those who are hopelessly in

---

[†] We use this spelling instead of the more common "holistic" to clearly communicate that we are talking about transformation of the *whole* person.

bondage. We open the community's eyes to environmental issues and help them see the importance of stewarding creation—and the benefits it can shower on them. In all things, we demonstrate the love of God to everyone as we work among them; through word and deed we proclaim truth and help people begin new lives as followers of Jesus Christ.

This is wholistic transformational development, the same mission that Jesus himself said he came to accomplish when he stood in the Temple and read this passage from the prophet Isaiah:

> The Spirit of the Lord is upon me,
>> because he has anointed me
>> to proclaim good news to the poor.
> He has sent me to proclaim liberty to the captives
>> and recovering of sight to the blind,
>> to set at liberty those who are oppressed,
> to proclaim the year of the Lord's favor.[1]

Jesus has commissioned us to the same work he did. He has called us to prayerfully walk among the poor and ask the Father to help us identify their felt needs and the root causes of those needs. We ask God to raise up strong pastors in the local churches who will have a heart for their people and the desire to see them transformed and living abundant lives in Christ. We pray for them to become joyful people of praise, oaks of righteousness to the glory of God.[2]

The Central and Vital Role of the Local Church

God's primary agent for transformation in the world is ordinary people gathered in community as the local church. The church is not just a group of like-minded followers of Jesus who have a heart for their neighbors; it is the supernatural bride of Christ, through whom he desires to transform communities.

To paraphrase Isaiah, we might say, "The Spirit of the Lord God is upon the local church, because the Lord has anointed her to bring good news to the poor; to bind up the brokenhearted, to proclaim liberty to the captives, and the opening of the prison to those who are bound; to proclaim the year of the Lord's favor."[3]

Our mission in Christ is to address brokenness in our world, release those who are bound, comfort those who are mourning, and exchange their sorrow for gladness and a spirit of praise; to build people up as priests of the Lord, a rejoicing community, established under the covenant of God.

Though many secular development organizations (and, sadly, some Christian agencies as well) *talk* about utilizing the people and resources of the local church in their development work, they fail to embrace the real reason why the church can be effective in its mission as agents of wholistic community transformation: It's because a vital local church is filled with the presence of the Holy Spirit, the real agent of all meaningful transformation.

Even with all its flaws, the church is God's chosen method for accomplishing his work on earth. We have seen transformational development occur in fragile communities, and they have become sustainable without ongoing outside assistance because of the presence and impact of an engaged local church.

The New Testament teaches us that as we are going throughout the world, we are to make disciples of those we meet. Those were Jesus' final instructions to his disciples.[4] He also taught that we are to love God with all our heart, soul, and mind—and that we are to love our neighbors as we love ourselves.[5] This love of our neighbor is especially focused on the poor, as we know that God defends the cause of the widow, orphan, immigrant, and refugee.[6]

Lasting Change

As those key issues that flow from the heart of God are present in our work in the world, we will see whole persons cared for, ministered to, and empowered to take ownership of their own development.

Individuals and communities will begin a new life marked by peace, justice, and righteousness.

In partnering with the local church, our desire is not to draw attention to ourselves, but to give all honor to the local church and all glory to God.

Occasionally, honor and favor spill over to us as well. In several instances, national governments have honored our programs and singled them out for recognition. Though we do not seek these accolades, they serve to demonstrate that wholistic transformational development changes lives and communities in sustainable, ongoing ways. Amazing doors can open, and amazing, transformational works can be accomplished, when God receives the glory in our lives and in our work. God's grace is released when we have an intimate relationship with him and when we trust his guidance and obey his call. He draws people to himself wherever he is honored and glorified. And he creates abundant good fruit—fruit that will last.

This section of the book will unpack some of the key guiding biblical principles at the heart of transformational development. As you explore the real meat of the book, we pray you will encounter and embrace new ways of pursuing lasting change in your community— whether it's around the world or across the street.

Questions for Reflection and Journaling

1. What has God taught you through this chapter? How has your concept of development changed through what we've shared?

2. How does the quote from Dr. Martin Luther King Jr. at the beginning of the chapter affect your view of wholistic transformation?

3. In what ways do you sense God is equipping you to help bring about transformational development and lasting change in the people he calls you to serve?

8

THE IMPORTANCE OF PRAYER

Prayer is not a monologue but a dialogue; God's voice in response to mine is its most essential part. Listening to God's voice is the secret of the assurance that He will listen to mine.

ANDREW MURRAY

Call to me and I will answer you, and will tell you great and hidden things that you have not known.

JEREMIAH 33:3

FLORENCE

I was gathering with the Kenyan staff at our office in Nairobi for a full day of prayer. We had just begun working in the huge Kibera slum, and we were overwhelmed by all the issues that needed to be addressed there. We wondered how God would use us to bring about sustainable transformation amid such deep systemic poverty and suffering. There was much to pray about and so much to be done; and we had little idea how we could ever see true sustainable transformation take root in that place.

A missionary who was serving in a nation that was officially closed to missionary work was with us as a visitor on our day of prayer. She asked us to pray for that country, a place none of us had visited. Some of us didn't even know where it was located. She told us many examples of barriers that had been erected to hinder the gospel from penetrating that nation. Yet despite those obstacles, a vibrant and growing underground church existed. She told us about the widespread poverty and the great need for development. Armed with this information, we went back to prayer. We all sensed the presence of the Lord, and the intensity of our corporate prayer was profound. People were on their knees in deep worship, acknowledging God and inviting him to meet the needs of the people in that closed country.

During a break time, some of the staff crowded around a map to see where the country was located and what countries bordered it. We spent time quizzing the visiting missionary about the needs of the church there. By the end of the morning, it was clear that the church in this nation would be at the top of our prayer agenda for that day. We would focus on that country's needs—even above all the urgent things we were dealing with in our home base of Kenya.

As our time of prayer came to a close and our guest prepared to leave, she came to me and shared a message that she believed the Lord wanted her to give me. She said, "God wants you and your friend to go to this country and hear him from there."

After she left, I thought about the message she had shared with me, and God placed on my mind a sense that any delayed obedience on my part would be *dis*obedience.

I went to my office and called Kenya Airways to see if they had flights into that closed country. The ticket agent told me, "As a matter of fact, we do; we have flights twice a week, on Tuesdays and Fridays." As we continued our conversation, I asked the agent if there was any chance we could obtain free tickets to travel to this country for humanitarian activity. Surprisingly, Kenya Airways offered us two complimentary tickets—for the very next day!

I was stunned by how quickly this opportunity was developing. We had first heard about the need just that morning. We had prayed and believed that God wanted us to focus on this nation. And then, that very same afternoon, God had provided free passage for us to visit that closed country.

The following morning, I found myself at Jomo Kenyatta International Airport with a dear friend, preparing to board a plane to take us to a very foreign and unfamiliar place.

Please understand, we hadn't done a thing to prepare; we had only prayed and fully believed that God was leading us to investigate what he was doing in that nation. We wanted to hear from him to discover what our role might be in his plan and how we might support the underground church we'd been hearing about and praying for.

The flight had a scheduled stop on the way to our destination, and all passengers were required to get off the plane while it was being refueled. My companion and I found a quiet corner in the transit lounge. We realized we had no idea what we would do when we got where we were going—we had no contacts, no hotel, no plans at all. So we sat together in the transit lounge, held hands, and prayed, "Lord, as we enter this country that we believe you have called us to, please guide our steps. Allow us to meet your people. You know who they are, Lord, so please speak to us and guide us."

As we've often received God's guidance, we both fully believed he would answer, and we expected it would be with an idea, a thought, or a sense of his leading. But we did not expect him to speak in the way he did.

While we were praying, my friend and I both heard a voice behind us clearly say, "Farah Ali at the World Bank building." We opened our eyes, thinking it must be another traveler in the boarding area talking about a friend, but as we looked around, we realized that nobody was close enough for us to have heard. In fact, we were the only ones still sitting in the waiting area who had not yet reboarded the plane. We had been praying so intently that we almost missed our flight!

We hurried to board the plane and continue the flight to our destination. As we sat in our seats, we looked at each other and whispered, "Did you hear that?" We had both clearly heard a voice behind us while we were praying, and we had both heard the exact same thing: "Farah Ali at the World Bank building."

During the remainder of the flight, we realized there were many things we didn't yet know, but we greatly anticipated that God was ordering our steps and opening doors before us.

As we prepared to land, the flight attendants handed out immigration entry cards for us to complete with our passport and travel information. In the space provided for our local address we wrote, "World Bank building," and for the name of our local contact we wrote, "Farah Ali."

In the arrivals area, we presented our entry cards and passports to the immigration officer, and he asked us to stand aside and wait. After clearing everyone else from our flight through immigration, they called us back to the desk. A supervisor was there by now, and the officers seemed to be discussing our case. The supervisor finally said in English, "Well, they are going to the World Bank building, and she is a medical doctor, so I think it's okay. Let them enter." And without any further questioning or delay, they stamped our passports, and we entered the country.

We took a cab to the World Bank building and decided we'd just go in and ask for Farah Ali. If nobody by that name was there, then at least we had made it into the country and we would pray to see how God would lead us from there.

When we arrived at the World Bank building—both of us praying silently as we entered the imposing structure and approached the front desk—the receptionist was occupied. Behind the reception area, a corridor extended back to a group of offices. I saw a woman walking from one office to the next, and when she looked up, our eyes met. Immediately, she stopped, turned, and walked quickly to the reception desk.

"These are my visitors," she announced, and ushered us past the receptionist. We never had to speak a word or sign the entrance log.

We followed the woman down the corridor and into her office. As soon as she closed the door, she fell to her knees, quietly worshiping God and thanking him for his faithfulness.

It was Farah Ali.[†]

He Had It All Planned

We later learned that Farah was one of the leaders of the underground church in this closed country. Her house church group had been praying fervently about the overwhelming poverty in their nation and asking God for guidance about how they could minister effectively to the people. God had spoken to them in their time of prayer and said he would be sending two women from another nation to teach them how to minister to the poor effectively in a way that glorified him.

Since then, the church had been waiting expectantly for us to arrive.

Farah told us that God had spoken to her just the previous day.

"Get ready, those two women are coming."

Farah simply and joyfully obeyed. She moved her children into one bedroom of their apartment and prepared the other room for the two people God was sending.

That morning, while she was on her way to work, a fellow believer came up to her and quietly said, "God spoke to me this morning that those two women are coming today."

Farah smiled and said, "Yes, last night he also spoke to me, so I prepared a room, and I am going to my office to wait for them. He showed me that they'll be coming to the bank." So the whole morning, she kept busy, walking from office to office, keeping an eye on the reception area so she would notice everyone who walked in. When we entered, God said to Farah, "Those are your guests." And her heart leapt within her.

We stayed with her all week. After we told her about our ministry,

---

[†] Not her real name.

she asked us to lead a transformational development vision seminar for the leaders of the underground church. When our time there concluded, they enthusiastically adopted the vision as their own and we began working together. A man in the church was selected to be that country's first director.

That's how the work in that closed-off country began, and now it is thriving! The churches there are growing rapidly; people are drawn by the Christians' love and compassion for the poor and vulnerable populations.

Even where you least expect it, in the darkest of situations and in the most closed countries, the church is there. God is able to preserve his people, a remnant who have not forsaken him, and against whom the very gates of hell cannot prevail.

Today, the government of that closed country has given national honor to the success of our development programs. By the grace of God, they have routinely renewed our organization's registration to work there. We have equipped the national believers and given them tools to empower the local church so they can do even more ministry on their own. They are branching out to take on even more public ministries, as the Lord leads them.

One small act of obedience has borne abundant fruit—more than a hundredfold.

But to be clear, it is still a very closed country. Christians there cannot be public about their faith and cannot share it openly with others—it would be too dangerous and would gravely affect the work of the church. Even so, the local church is continuing to grow rapidly. For safety, they have limited the size of their small house-church groups to eight members each. Once a house church, or cell group, reaches that size, they disband. In anticipation of this moment, each member has been actively discipled and taught how to disciple others, so as the group separates, each member becomes responsible to start a new group and begin discipling the new believers who attend, preparing them for the time when the new group grows to eight members, and they go out to form eight new house church groups. Organic multiplication—that is how they are growing! Today, more baptisms are happening in that country than ever before.

God Still Speaks Today

We knew it before our initial trip to that country, but we experienced it there like never before: *God still speaks today!* He communicates with his people in various ways—sometimes through Scripture, sometimes through a word from someone else, and other times by a thought or mental image. Or, as we found in that airport lounge, it could be through an audible voice. The method isn't all that important, but the *message* always is. If we spend time with God in prayer, seek his direction, and listen for his reply, he will answer. Our task then is simply to obey.

I've found that I'm better able to hear or sense God's direction if I'm in a constant state of prayer. Scripture tells us to "pray without ceasing."[1] That doesn't mean we must always be on our knees in prayer, but that our hearts are in an ongoing dialogue with God, open to hear his direction and ready to obey him quickly.

God is a very strategic planner. He is always at work to fulfill his plans and purposes. He continually seeks people who are willing to be involved in his plan for the world. When we seek him, we will marvel at what he has in store.

Over the years, Charlie and I have both learned the importance of total obedience to God in following his promptings, regardless of what the circumstances or situations might dictate. Prayer is the *first* of our transformation principles—and for good reason. It is foundational to our life in Christ and our work for him. And it is a key ingredient to our becoming the kind of people God can use to truly make a difference in the world—as we learn to obey him and walk in relationship with him.

Prayer Brings Transformation

Prayer is the foundation for everything we do. It is both our primary principle and our practice for transformation. It is where we wage our greatest battles. People are transformed through prayer, and only transformed people can implement transformation in others.

Every ministry that seeks to be an effective agent of God's work in the world must not only fully understand the importance of prayer, but also actively practice it. Jesus said, "My house shall be called a house of prayer."[2] For the local church, there is nothing more powerful than ministry fueled by a furnace of prayer. Everything we do must be birthed in prayer, nourished in prayer, and sustained in prayer.

We pray to express our complete dependence on God, and we pray to block the strategies our adversary uses to tempt us, destroy us, and ruin our ministry and effectiveness for God's work.

Prayer is not just us speaking to God. He also wants to speak to us. It's a two-way conversation. Not only do we share our hearts with God, but we must also learn how to *listen* for his voice. We may be so anxious to *do something*—to fix a problem such as poverty—that we rush in before determining what *God* wants us to do. It is vital that we spend time with God—*being* with him before attempting to *do* anything for him.

Being versus Doing

Being is stillness, but it's *not* inactivity. It is the settled state in which we actively seek God's wisdom, insight, and guidance—where we listen more than we speak. But stillness of heart and mind, and seeking God's direction, take time. We must master the part of our human nature that constantly wants to be *doing* something to solve problems as soon as we encounter them. Just as Jesus was never in a hurry, we must be willing to invest ample time simply *being* in God's presence so we can hear what *he* desires, know his heart for the populations we are serving, and understand how *he* wants the *doing* accomplished.

As action-oriented people who want to bring about change, we often bounce up from our knees and immediately get busy doing what seems best to us. Our organizations seldom say, "Let's pause for the next week and seek God and ask what he wants us to do next year." Instead, we often start a planning meeting with a short prayer, fully believing we already know what God has called us to do and what our next steps will be—even what our ten-year plan looks like. But if that is how we seek God's guidance, it's no wonder there are so many failed missions projects abandoned by people who really thought they were doing God's will, but were actually just rushing ahead at full speed, doing what they thought best.

The Life In Abundance team has experienced firsthand what can happen when an organization makes prayer a priority. As I've mentioned, our staff gathers every Monday for an extended time of corporate prayer, in addition to our daily devotions. Most staff members also fast for the entire day. Our practice is to set aside the first day of every workweek to seek God, bring him our concerns and the needs from each of the nations where we are working, and listen for his wisdom and guidance. Great fruit has come from this. We've realized that prayer is the "greater work" we must be doing.

Southeast Christian Church has likewise made it a priority for their missions staff to stay informed about what's going on in the world—and then pray about it together. Charlie and I have often shared with each other that praying with our staff is like the secret ingredient: When you get that one thing right, everything else seems to fall into place.

How to Pray and Hear from God

One of the most important things to learn as a disciple is how to be led by the Spirit of God. If my travel companion and I had not been comfortable asking God for guidance, believing he would answer, and then listening to receive it, we might not have heard his response while we were sitting in the airport waiting to reboard our flight.

Being led by God's Spirit requires that we know God's voice, that we wait quietly and expectantly for his direction, and that we are ready to obey it when we receive it.

Most of us are familiar with talking to God in prayer. But prayer is so much more than talking to God; it is also a time to allow his Spirit to communicate with us. If our prayers consist only of our talking, ending with "amen," and then going about our day, we'll likely never hear what God has to say. Simply stated, we cannot hear unless we take time to *listen*.

There is a practice called *seeking prayer* or *listening prayer* that can help us quiet our minds, silence disruptions, put the world on hold, and allow God to speak to us. Disciples sometimes call this practice "waiting on God," and I like that phrase because it reminds us that God is in charge. We relinquish our deadlines and fast-paced schedules to wait expectantly for God to impart his wisdom.

God wants to reveal himself to you. Pray and wait, believing it will happen. Use the Scriptures to quiet your mind. "Seek first the kingdom of God and his righteousness, and all these things will be added to you."[3]

Throughout the Bible, we find examples of people hearing from God in silence and solitude.

God spoke to Elijah, for example, not in the wind, the earthquake, or the fire—but in "the sound of a low whisper."[4] David tells us, "Ponder in your own hearts on your beds, and be silent."[5] And God instructs us through the sons of Korah, "Be still, and know that I am God."[6]

Jesus, our model for how to live our lives in connection with God's Spirit, often stole away to quiet places where he could converse with his Father. One of the first things the Gospel of Mark tells us about Jesus is that "rising very early in the morning, while it was still dark, he departed and went out to a desolate place, and there he prayed."[7]

Sometimes when you wait in silence for God, you will feel his peaceful presence. Other times, he may bring a passage of Scripture to mind, or perhaps a song, an idea, an impression, or a picture.

Sometimes, silence will be all you get. That's okay; you didn't fail, and it's not a waste of time. Remember, you are waiting for God. He is in control. It isn't your responsibility to come away with a profound insight or a call to action. Rather, your job is to build your ability to quiet your heart and your mind so you can hear God's Spirit. He's teaching you patience and how to listen. And if you determine to keep spending time in "seeking prayer," God may make himself known to you in ways you cannot anticipate.

Knowledge, wisdom, and guidance come from being in God's presence. They come from regular time spent seeking him in prayer; and they come from knowing God's Word and basing your life on *his* standard.

One thing to avoid is waiting on God, seeking him, listening for his direction, and then saying, "Thank you" and "Amen" and popping up right away to get busy doing something else. Another danger is thinking that everything we hear is from God, even when it is not in alignment with what the written Word of God already says. God does not contradict himself. So spending time both reading the Bible and praying are two important disciplines in every Christian's life.

We may see ourselves as "on mission" to *do* something for God. But he would prefer that our priority be getting to know him and becoming like him. That kind of relationship comes only by spending daily time *seeking* him.

The goal of everything in our lives must be intimacy with God—not seeking to be active on his behalf; not engaging in effective ministry; but simply being, waiting, listening, and yearning for closeness with him.

Charlie and I have a friend with a high-level job in global ministry who spends time every morning sitting in the same chair by the same window, reading his Bible and praying. He says that he stays in that chair until he hears something from God each day.

We have found that the most fruitful ministries are those that make prayer their number one priority. Listening prayer, or seeking prayer, shouldn't be the only type of prayer we employ throughout the day, but it is an important part of a good prayer life—waiting in stillness, solitude, and silence with God, without asking for anything except his presence, his voice, and his guidance. There is an affinity between the human spirit and God's Spirit, but it takes listening, waiting, and seeking for that connection to develop. So sit and wait, and see what God will do.

Questions for Reflection and Journaling

1. How can you better incorporate prayer into your daily life? When, where, and how can you make prayer more of a priority?

2. Have you ever sensed the Spirit of God speaking to you through a hunch, a picture, a Bible verse, or a song? How did you respond?

3. Why is it worthwhile to spend daily time with God—in prayer and in his Word?

4. Is there something you sense God has been laying on your heart or wanting to get across to you? Do you sense that he is calling you to something? What is it, and how or why do you have this sense?

9

LIVING WITH AN ETERNAL PERSPECTIVE

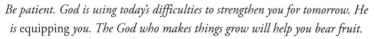

Be patient. God is using today's difficulties to strengthen you for tomorrow. He is equipping you. The God who makes things grow will help you bear fruit.
MAX LUCADO

You did not choose me, but I chose you and appointed you that you should go and bear fruit and that your fruit should abide.
JOHN 15:16

FLORENCE

I was serving in a Nairobi women's prison medical clinic during my first year of marriage. Because it was early in my medical career, I also took on extra shifts in the surgical ward of a prestigious private hospital to gain experience.

While on duty one evening, I admitted a patient, whom I will call Kamau, who was in his late sixties and had symptoms of abdominal cancer. He was weak, and there were clear indications that the disease had likely progressed to a late stage.

There was something about Kamau that strongly reminded me of my father. I could not place it—perhaps it was his demeanor, age, voice, or how he treated me. I couldn't be certain. But during the hour I spent recording his medical history on his intake chart, I found my heart full of compassion and concern for him.

After consulting with the chief surgeon, we compiled a list of tests for Kamau to undergo. I explained each one to him before leaving for the night. The following evening, when I got to the ward, the nurses told me Kamau had asked for me during the day. When I went to check on him, he wanted to know whether his test results were back yet. I went through his file, updating him where possible, and we talked about his treatment as I assured him that he would be kept comfortable and informed.

By the third day, his condition had stabilized, and surgery was planned to arrest some internal bleeding and deal with an intestinal obstruction. Kamau wanted to know whether I would be in the operating room, and when I told him I would be there, he relaxed and was thankful. Because the disease was already quite advanced, I told him that this procedure was intended to improve his quality of life rather than cure him. Talking to a patient about end-of-life issues is never easy, and because he still reminded me of my father, his situation was becoming emotional for me. I kept praying that somehow he would be healed.

Just before Kamau went under anesthesia, I squeezed his hand, and he smiled. The surgical procedure began, and to my deep disappointment the findings were disheartening. There were several areas of bleeding that could not be controlled. The cancer had spread, and it was impossible to resolve the intestinal obstruction. After concluding that not much could be done, we began the closing suturing. Kamau was given only a few days to live.

When I arrived at the hospital the following day, I heard that Kamau was awake and asking for me. I dreaded having to give him the disappointing update, yet I had promised to keep him informed.

Taking his hand as I sat next to his bed, I told him that the operation had not been successful, and I was sorry that we could not do more to help him. I told him it was the surgeon's opinion that he had only a few days to live. He gave me a weary smile and held on to my hand. He thanked me for sharing the good news. I thought he was confused or had not heard me properly, so I explained it again, this time more clearly and directly.

Kamau assured me he had heard and understood me well the first time. He repeated that this was good news and told me not to be sad. He said that he had loved, served, and lived for God for many years, and he had been looking forward with eagerness to the time when he would see Jesus face-to-face. The news I had shared with him meant the time had finally come, and he would soon see his Savior—so he saw it as very good news. He then turned the conversation to me, and in an endearing way, referring to me as his daughter, he asked whether I knew Jesus and if I was living for him fully, without any doubt or compromise.

He had my attention. I knew God as a Father and as a friend. I had totally surrendered my life to him, but I certainly did not have the close relationship with God that Kamau enjoyed. We talked at length. I cried openly during this conversation, and as we finished, I gave him a hug and said good night.

When I came back to the hospital the following morning, Kamau had already passed away; it did not take as long as expected. I was the doctor covering the first shift, so I was the one to certify his death. His face was peaceful, with a half-smile. As I signed the death certificate, I was certain he was with the one he loved.

Time to Reevaluate My Life

My experience with Kamau taught me many things I still treasure in my heart. One of the most important lessons I learned through that dear man was to live with an eternal perspective—looking at day-to-day actions and decisions in light of their eternal value, and measuring them with the yardstick of heaven. I had a new realization that it is possible for a child of God to walk through this life and remain focused and intentional to the very end. Kamau showed me that the number of our days is uncertain, and that life passes quickly. Knowing that, I need to invest my life wisely in things that matter for eternity. I also became aware that it is very easy to get caught up in the business of life and to lose focus. I determined that I would regularly stop and take time to reevaluate my life, and make necessary adjustments quickly.

I learned that life is best lived with a long-term view—not going through life thinking of what I would enjoy most today, but rather using God's values to measure every day's events and decisions, knowing that everything I choose to do or think has an eternal consequence.

Jesus taught this perspective when he told his followers not to store up treasure in this world, but in heaven—"for where your treasure is, there your heart will be also."[1] In my walk with the Lord, I have learned that earthly treasures compete with God's purpose for our lives. We must choose to stay close to his purpose, guarding it and treasuring the Kingdom of Heaven.

In the book of Proverbs, a father instructs his sons based on the wisdom he has accumulated over the span of his lifetime: "Above all else, guard your heart, for everything you do flows from it."[2] The heart is where our eternal treasure is held, and it influences who we are, what we do, and to whom we belong. Jesus makes it very clear when he says, "The good person out of the good treasure of his heart produces good, and the evil person out of his evil treasure produces evil, for out of the abundance of the heart his mouth speaks."[3] What's in your heart matters. I understood that truth from a young age, but I came to *know* it fully as I watched Kamau prepare to pass from this life into the arms of his heavenly Father.

We cannot allow anything to enter our hearts that is not of God, and we must not allow anything—any possession, relationship, dream, or plan—to take the place that rightfully belongs to God.

Resting on God's Promises

God has promised to always be with us. He has promised to care for us as he cares for the birds of the air.[4] I've found that living with an eternal perspective is impossible if I do not rest on God's promises. Failure to trust in his unfathomable love and believe he will keep his promises leads to anxiety, as we foolishly attempt to watch out for ourselves, in case he does not. He reassuringly tells us not to worry about the necessities of life. In the Sermon on the Mount, Jesus says, "The Gentiles seek after all these things [what to eat, drink, and wear], and your heavenly Father knows that you need them all. But seek first the kingdom of God and his righteousness, and all these things will be added to you."[5]

If you live with an eternal perspective, you will have less anxiety about the future. Your heart and mind will be focused on the one who holds the future and who holds you in his mighty, compassionate hands.

This doesn't mean you won't encounter obstacles or problems as you go through life. Jesus told his disciples, "I have said these things to you, that in me you may have peace. In the world you will have tribulation. But take heart; I have overcome the world."[6] And he explained, "If the world hates you, know that it has hated me before it hated you. . . . If they persecuted me, they will also persecute you."[7]

Though we can expect opposition as we fulfill our calling, as our hearts and minds filter everything through an eternal perspective, we can be encouraged by Paul, who was no stranger to violent opposition and hardship. He writes, "We do not lose heart. Though our outer self is wasting away, our inner self is being renewed day by day. For this light momentary affliction is preparing for us an eternal weight of glory beyond all comparison, as we look not to the things that are seen but to the things that are unseen. For the things that are seen are transient, but the things that are unseen are eternal."[8]

Kamau was joyfully looking forward to the things that are unseen. He modeled for me what life could look like—eagerly and expectantly looking forward to seeing God face to face.

This World Is Not Our Home

I learned what it means to admit we are strangers on earth and that our home is in heaven—that we are to live fully while on this planet, yet eagerly look forward to meeting our Savior. An eternal perspective helps us remember who we are, and it reminds us not to become conformed to the mold of this world. It gives us a godly outlook on success and significance.

Keeping an eternal perspective sets our hearts free and gives us rest. Worry has no place in our minds. Our focus in this present life is clarified. Our ambition is to seek God's Kingdom; his righteousness becomes our priority. If we are granted material prosperity, worldly status, accolades, and rewards, we do not allow them to compromise our allegiance to our Father.

We maintain this posture by a lifestyle of nonconformity, in which we consciously choose to align with the good, pleasing, and perfect will of God—continually offering our lives as a living sacrifice to him.[9]

Why It Matters

With more than three billion people in the world still unreached by the gospel,[10] we must approach our missions work with an eternal perspective in mind. It's important to be certain we are accomplishing something of lasting value and that we continually scrutinize our work, asking ourselves, "Is our ministry investment bearing fruit that will last?"

I urge you to regularly stop and evaluate your life and work with an eternal perspective in mind. Look at the journey of your life, see what the Lord has invested in you to prepare you, and how you're using it. Carve out significant times—such as your birthday or your ministry's anniversary—to evaluate your choices and what you've accomplished, and assess its value in light of eternity. After you look back, look ahead at the things you believe God has prepared for you to do, and make any adjustments needed to bring your life and ministry into alignment with God's will and more fit for his service. The apostle Paul puts it this way: "Walk in a manner worthy of the Lord, fully pleasing to him: bearing fruit in every good work."[11]

Questions for Reflection and Journaling

1. If you fully believed that God would provide for your needs, if you truly sought first the Kingdom of God, what would change in your life?

2. Looking back at your life's journey from an eternal perspective, how do your actions and decisions measure up? What changes do you need to make to ensure that your actions really matter for eternity?

3. What activities are you involved in now that will bear lasting fruit? Is there anything that has gone unchecked in your life? What keeps you from fully serving and obeying God?

10

LOVING THE WHOLE PERSON

*I want to be generous with my affection and patience and
love unconditionally. It is easier to love a person with their
flaws than to weed through them. I want to love the whole
person, not parts; and this is how I want to be loved.*

JEWEL KILCHER

*And Jesus increased in wisdom and in stature
and in favor with God and man.*

LUKE 2:52

FLORENCE

I knocked on the door hesitantly, reviewing in my mind the correct
Amharic greeting to use if anyone answered. Part of my daily practice
in Ethiopia was to meet someone new in the community and have a
conversation with them.

Soon a woman with a small questioning smile came to the door. I
quickly guessed she was in her thirties. I also couldn't help but notice
her disfigured nose and other obvious symptoms of leprosy.

I smiled and greeted her, and after a few moments of exchanging
pleasantries, she invited me in for tea. Of course I accepted. Entering
her small home, I noticed she didn't have much of anything. In
fact, she didn't have a propane burner or any kind of fire on which
to cook.

I watched her hobble on feet deformed by years of leprosy-caused injuries as she went next door to ask a neighbor to borrow her burner and kettle. She stopped at the next house to get some water and ask for some tea. She returned, clutching the borrowed ingredients in her scarred hands. I helped her make the tea, and we talked while the water heated.

Fortunately, I had brought along sugar and bread, which I had planned to leave as a gift. But now we could sit together, drink our tea, and talk as I practiced my elementary-level Amharic.

Looking back on that visit, I think she was just being polite when she asked me in for tea. I don't think she expected me to actually accept her invitation. There was a stigma associated with leprosy, and it was a bit unusual for someone who did not have the disease to socialize with someone who did. But there we were, talking and drinking tea for about two hours.

Her name was Almaz, and her husband had died of AIDS. She had two children, ages five and seven, but they weren't home while I was there—they were out begging. I told her about myself, that I was a doctor from Kenya and was in Ethiopia attending language school so I could practice medicine among those in the community who had leprosy. I also told her about Jesus and how my life had been changed by following him.

As I was preparing to leave and we were saying our goodbyes, I gave her a hug. As I did, she started crying, and then began sobbing deeply. I wasn't sure what she was going through, but it seemed as if she had not been hugged in a very long time—if ever. She clung to me, continuing to weep, and held me so tightly that I honestly thought my ribs would break. My medical training kicked in and I wondered whether the disease had robbed her hands of the sense of feeling so she didn't realize how tightly she was gripping me.

She didn't let go for the longest time. She just sobbed and squeezed. It was as if she feared that if she released her grip, I might go away and never come back. I could feel the years of emotional pain in her body and could only imagine what she had been through as an outcast living with her disease. I sensed the heavy burden she carried as the one person responsible for her children and their future. As we continued to embrace, I think she truly felt loved—perhaps for the first time.

The next day, she came to our house and brought her two children so I could meet them. Almaz and I became friends, and we got together maybe once a week during my time there. I would drop in at her house, and we'd talk and have tea.

Through our time together, she came to know Christ so beautifully. She was baptized and became part of the local church. But though her life was changing, she still relied on income from her children's begging to take care of the family's needs.

When the church started a table bank, Almaz joined. A table bank is a member-owned-and-operated savings and credit group, which teaches members the importance of wise money management and strategies for creating income-generating activities. Almaz learned a lot through the training and started thinking about ways she could earn money through a small business. At first it was hard for her to find any money to invest in the group, but soon she took out a small loan from the table bank and started a business.

The changes in her life soon became evident to everyone around her. She was happy being part of the church and the table bank group. She realized she was appreciated and loved, and as a result she became more self-confident. Soon she was able to enroll her children in school, since she no longer needed them to be on the streets begging for money at stoplights.

Her transformation began when I refused to see my relationship with her as only an opportunity to practice a new language. I was genuinely interested in who she was, what she felt her true needs were, and whether she had a relationship with Jesus. She sensed my love and concern for her as a whole person, and her transformation grew from that simple cup of borrowed tea.

Wholistic Means Caring for the Whole Person

Our focus in the work of transformational development is to create long-lasting, sustainable change in the total person and in all parts of the community. Almaz truly experienced total transformation! Spiritually, she was saved and baptized; physically, she was able to earn money to take care of her family and manage her disease; emotionally, she felt loved and appreciated; and socially, she made new friends and felt part of a supportive group.

Jesus is our model for ministry. Just as he showed concern for the whole person, he wants us also to be concerned with wholistic development in people's lives. God cares about our emotional health, our physical needs, our emotional strength, and our social interaction. He's not focused only on the final destination of our souls. His all-consuming love and concern reach out to each of us in our need, just as he reached out to every need that Almaz experienced.

God opened our eyes at Life In Abundance to the concept of loving the *whole* person. We call it the Three C's. It's very simple:

1. The first *C* is the *Great Commandment*, found in Matthew 22, Mark 12, and Luke 10—to love God with all our heart, soul, and mind, and to love our neighbor as ourselves.

2. The second *C* is the *Great Commission*, from Matthew 28, where we are told to disciple people around the world, teaching them to obey everything God has commanded.

3. The third *C* is the *Great Concern*, from Matthew 25, where Jesus says, "I was hungry and you gave me food, I was thirsty and you gave me drink, I was a stranger and you welcomed me, I was naked and you clothed me, I was sick and you visited me, I was in prison and you came to me."[1] Anytime we enter a community or we're trying to help people, they have a felt need. That's what the Great Concern deals with—addressing that felt need.

The Great Commission and the Great Concern flow naturally from the Great Commandment. But we need all three; otherwise our ministry is unbalanced, unable to do the work it was intended to accomplish. Global North churches and missions organizations often make the mistake of segmenting these ministries—that is, they focus on one at the expense or exclusion of the others. Some churches are all about evangelism and discipleship; others go all-in caring for people with great physical or mental health needs. The Great Concern speaks to seeing people in need and helping them with those needs. But we don't stop there. For example, take international adoption: How could the situation be so dire in a community that they would give up their next generation? Adoption to a more developed country helps the individual child, but it is not a long-term solution. There are too many impoverished children around the world. A more wholistic—and long-term—approach is to strengthen the churches in those communities and teach them how to care for these vulnerable children.

The Great Commission, Great Commandment, and Great Concern are naturally interrelated. We address the felt need (Great Concern), disciple the church in addressing the root causes that created the need (Great Commission), and all of this is an act of worship for our Creator (Great Commandment). If we're busy feeding the hungry and giving clean water to the thirsty, but we're not paying equal attention to their spiritual well-being—or we're discipling them in the ways they need to grow, but not meeting their physical and emotional needs—then we're doing only a partial job of loving God and loving our neighbor. Love compels us to do something, and the demonstration of loving God is loving our neighbor.

Until we become aware that each person needs to receive ministry in each of these three areas, we're not really fulfilling the gospel. If we focus only on the Great Commission, we run the risk of making people feel that the only part of them that matters is their soul—that God doesn't really care about their other needs. And if our focus is solely on the Great Concern, we might be so busy helping meet physical needs and fighting for social justice that we never ask about a person's relationship with God.

But we don't live segmented lives—our physical well-being is linked with our spiritual health, and it all relates to our love for God and our neighbor. We were not created as compartmentalized beings, and we must have the needs of the whole person in mind as we minister to people, all of whom were created in God's image.

As churches or ministries specialize in any one of these three areas, their efficacy in seeing lives or communities transformed diminishes. For example, they may teach on Sunday how to love God and be kind to people in their lives, but then never challenge people to grow deeper in their relationship with God or to love others through their actions. Instead, they outsource the Great Commission to church-planting missionaries. And while they're teaching about love, people in the community may be unemployed and hungry. The Great Concern gets outsourced to a soup kitchen or a child sponsorship program or a prison ministry.

Wholistic Disciple-Making

The normal Christian life comes from discipling the whole person—not just teaching people how to study the Bible and how to love God, but also teaching them how to provide for their families, how to maintain good health, and how to avoid bad financial practices.

The Three C's may be seen as a progression. The first words of the Great Commission are often translated as "Go therefore and make disciples of all nations," but a more literal translation of the Greek verb forms would be "*As you are going*, disciple all the nations." Often we are given the idea that "Go" is an imperative, the important part of this directive. But "going" is something we're already doing. Think in terms of "as you are going about your daily lives." That is the context here.

The Three C's work together as a progression: As you are loving the Lord your God with all your heart, soul, and strength, also love the people around you (as you love yourself). And as you are loving God and people, put that love into action—providing them with food, water, clothes, and shelter; welcoming them in if they don't have a safe place to live; bringing healing to the sick; and not neglecting those in prison. Listen to their side of the story and work for justice. Then, as you go about your daily life, disciple the people around you, teaching them how to fulfill the Great Commandment, the Great Commission, and the Great Concern. In this way, the impact of your ministry will continue to grow, multiplying itself to an even larger area of influence.

Who Is Your Neighbor?

In Luke 10, an expert in the law asks Jesus how to obtain eternal life. Jesus replies by asking him what the law says about it. In response, the lawyer recites the Great Commandment: "You shall love the Lord your God with all your heart and with all your soul and with all your strength and with all your mind, and your neighbor as yourself." But then, as if looking for a legal loophole, he asks Jesus, "And who is my neighbor?"

Jesus then tells a story, which has become known as the parable of the good Samaritan:

A man traveling from Jerusalem to Jericho was attacked by robbers and left for dead on the side of the road. Three other travelers were making the same trip and came upon the scene of the crime. First, a priest arrived and saw the severely injured man, but he passed on the other side of the road. Later, a Levite came along and saw the man, and he also walked past on the other side of the road. Then along came a Samaritan, an outsider, part of an ethnic group that was distrusted and hated by the Jews. He stopped to help the injured man. He tended to the man's wounds, found a place for him to receive further care, and paid for his expenses.[2]

This parable highlights two people to whom the questioning lawyer would have been able to relate: a priest and a Levite—both of whom would have been experts in the law. The priest was higher in status and authority than the lawyer, and the Levite was more of an equal. Both men failed to uphold the law by showing love to the injured traveler.

In his telling of the story, Jesus points out that the robbers had stripped the victim of his clothes and left him half dead. In that culture, two primary ways that one could determine a stranger's nationality and status were by their clothing and their accent. But both of these had been taken away from the injured man. It was impossible to know at a glance whether he was a "somebody" or a "nobody"—a Jew, a Samaritan, or someone from another culture. And there was no way to know whether he had any social, political, or religious standing. All identifiers had been stripped away—he was just a beaten, robbed, half-dead traveler.

Two men well versed in God's law did not respond as the Great Commandment required—by loving the injured man as themselves. Instead, a person whom the Jews disdained, someone who would have been considered an enemy, showed compassion for the man by stopping, cleaning and bandaging his wounds, transporting him to a safe place, and personally caring for him. The next day, he arranged for ongoing care for the man and provided payment for it.

Jesus asked the lawyer which of the three passersby was a "neighbor" to the injured man. The man answered correctly: "The one who showed him mercy." And Jesus said to him, "You go, and do likewise."[3]

Our neighbor is anyone with whom we can share God's love. We don't get to choose our neighbors. They don't have to be similar to us, or make us comfortable, or have the same skin color, or speak the same language we do. Our neighbor is anyone God places in our path.

The love we are to show to others must be without judgment or precondition. We are to love people by genuinely seeking what is best for them. Loving our neighbors means loving the whole person by attending to their needs—physical, emotional, relational, and spiritual.

Loving our neighbors includes those who are mean, unkind, ungrateful, and who seem like enemies to us. When we begin with hearts that first—and fully—love God, we are able to live out God's unselfish, relentless, never-ending, unconditional love. This is the biblical basis for effective wholistic ministry. It's how—and why—we love and minister to the whole person.

Don't Stop with the Obvious Needs

One day soon after I moved with my family to Ethiopia, a young girl who was about seven years old fainted on the street outside our mission compound. The people in the community knew I was a medical doctor, and immediately someone rushed to find me and insisted I go look at the girl. When I arrived at her side and began checking her vital signs, it was obvious she was hypoglycemic. So I asked someone to run to the closest store and get a bottle of soft drink. After drinking some of the sugary drink, the girl quickly came around. She was still a bit confused, but she started talking. And she kept repeating a phrase. As I was still learning the Amharic language, I asked the people standing around, "What is she saying?"

"She says it wasn't her turn."

I discovered that the girl's parents both suffered from leprosy, and they would stand on street corners in the capital city, begging for food. Every evening, they brought home whatever they had received. It was never very much, so they fed their two children by turns—one child would eat today, the other would eat tomorrow, and the cycle would repeat. The little girl had fainted because it wasn't her turn to eat that day.

I kept the girl with me for the rest of the day. I brought her to the mission compound and to my home. We got word to her parents, and they came to us that evening. I met them, and I started to understand what they did to survive and why they did it. I connected them to the local church so they could be part of a program that ministered to the needs of beggars.

In addition to helping them earn money so they could feed their family, the church taught them about Jesus and his love for them. They were loved, cared for, and discipled. That one act of responding in wholistic love to a family of total outcasts changed the entire trajectory of their lives. The girl became healthy and did well at school. Eventually, she went on to college. I believe she still teaches Sunday school in that church today.

This is just one example of what can happen when we love the whole person and love our neighbors as ourselves. It begins with a concern, goes on to a command, and leads to a commission to disciple people so they, in turn, can help others.

If our only task were to preach the message of salvation, we could have revived the girl, told her about Jesus, asked her to pray with us, and then sent her on her way for someone else to pick up the baton and run the next part of the race with her. Had we done that, she might have died on the streets. But thankfully, we realized that our work wasn't summed up only in the Great Commission. It included the Great Commandment and the Great Concern as well. And it's brilliant how well they all work together!

Jesus Was a Whole Person

We usually think of Jesus as an adult, teaching his disciples and doing miracles. But he was born as a baby boy and grew up in a family with a mother, father, and siblings. Jesus did kid things when he was a kid, and he learned important life skills from his parents and those around him.

Luke 2:52 gives us an inside look at God's concern for the whole person. It says, "Jesus increased in wisdom and in stature and in favor with God and man." We typically don't think about God *growing*, but

Jesus was God incarnate—fully God and yet fully man. Luke says that Jesus increased, or grew, in several ways:

- in wisdom—that is, in his intellect and skills;
- in stature—which speaks of his physical body and health;
- in favor with God—which means increasing in spiritual understanding, discernment, and ministry;
- in favor with man—which means he learned how to interact with people, gain acceptance, and remain in their good graces.

We see in this one story God's concern with all areas of our lives—spiritual, physical, emotional, and social.

Just as Jesus showed throughout his ministry, we must have a wholistic concern for our neighbors. The Three C's are a great reminder of how Jesus taught us to love and serve.

Questions for Reflection and Journaling

1. Is there someone God has put in your path who is difficult to love and care for? What would you do differently if you truly believed God wanted you to love this person wholistically?

2. Which of the Three C's are you most focused on, perhaps to the exclusion of one or both of the others? How can you change that behavior with a new perspective?

3. Do the Three C's challenge your theology? What do you sense God is leading you to do right now?

11

USING RELIEF AND DEVELOPMENT WISELY

*If we treat only the symptoms or if we misdiagnose the
underlying problem, we will not improve their situation,
and we might actually make their lives worse.*

STEVE CORBETT AND BRIAN FIKKERT, *WHEN HELPING HURTS*

You shall love your neighbor as yourself.

MATTHEW 22:39

CHARLIE

Imagine you are walking through a forest and hear some people shouting. They sound panicky, so you pick up your pace and follow their voices. The shouts grow louder until you come upon a deep hole in the ground. Inside the hole is a group of people who have fallen in and can't climb out. It appears they've been down there for some time.

It's obvious they are very weak and desperately in need of food and water. You throw your water bottle down and assure them you'll be back with more. A few hours later, you return with more bottles of water and some food. The people are very grateful. Next, you realize that with the sun setting, it will soon be cold, so you run off to get blankets, along with more food and water.

You continue to bring food, water, and other supplies for several days, and it's clear that the people in the deep hole are feeling much better. Their energy has increased to the point where they are trying to devise ways to climb out of the hole. It makes you happy to see that you have helped them survive and recover their strength so quickly.

Finally, you take time to engage them in conversation, trying to understand why they were walking in the forest in the first place and how they happened to fall into the deep hole. Eventually, one of the people becomes exasperated and says, "While we have certainly appreciated the food, water, and blankets, what we could really use is a tall ladder so we can climb out of this hole and go home."

You were so focused on providing vital supplies to help them with their immediate needs that you neglected their long-term need to *get out of the hole.*

When Humane Relief Becomes Inhumane

Of course it's humane to give these people emergency aid when the need is so critical. But if you continue to provide the same aid repeatedly after the immediate need has been taken care of, the same help becomes inhumane—because you're not helping; you're prolonging the problem. After the initial needs have been met, it's time to bring the ladder to help get them out of the hole and get on with life.

Countries like Haiti have been in a deep hole for a long time, and humanitarian aid agencies have provided a seemingly endless supply of emergency resources. So many well-intentioned people and organizations—and even nations—are working very hard, investing fortunes, but are not seeing lasting results from their efforts. Instead of helping the Haitians climb out of the hole, they are basically throwing their resources into a hole.

If it were our aim to help Haiti rise up to financial independence, we would have a ladder standing by—so the moment they had the strength to climb it, they could escape their problem. Yes, emergency aid is needed. But ladders are also needed. The local church can build the ladders to help people climb out of the holes they find themselves in.

The Danger of Dependency

We all like to fix problems; it makes us feel good. People thank us, and we can stand a bit taller. But attempting to fix the problem of poverty with charitable gifts, sponsorships, or shipments of emergency aid can actually do more to promote dependency than it does to solve the core problem. Without building a relationship that addresses the whole person and is focused on lasting transformation, such help ignores the recipient's ability and reduces their self-reliance.

The apostle Paul said, "Let us not grow weary of doing good, for in due season we will reap, if we do not give up. So then, as we have opportunity, let us do good to everyone, and especially to those who are of the household of faith."[1] Compassion is at the very heart of the character of God. As Christians, we are called to love our neighbor as we love ourselves[2]—it's a vital part of our evangelistic witness. Especially if they are brothers and sisters in Christ, love compels us to reach out to help them. However, when "compassionate action" becomes merely a business model, a fundraising appeal, or a strategy for evangelism and church growth, it loses much of its essential quality of unconditional love.

Relief and/or Development?

Two terms often heard together in humanitarian aid efforts are *relief* and *development*. They have almost become a phrase, like "ham and eggs" or "bread and butter," denoting two things that naturally go together. But in the case of relief and development, they are actually two very different activities.

Relief is a free, no-strings-attached handout of vital supplies, given in the immediate aftermath of a disaster or an unforeseen emergency. The intent of relief is to quickly save lives that are in dire peril. However, once the immediate emergency has passed, the relief must cease, or else it can delay or inhibit the rebuilding process in the community.

Development is a process by which a community is empowered to identify and carry out long-term sustainable solutions for its own needs. The result is increased capacity and dignity for everyone involved. As we mentioned in chapter 7, we believe in going beyond the practice of development to work for "wholistic transformational development," a process that involves the entire person—and entire communities—and results in lasting change.

Relief Is Addictive

If the route to sustainable transformational development is such an obviously better choice over ongoing emergency relief efforts, why do we not see it implemented more often and successfully in needy communities around the world?

One reason is that when affluent people see a need, providing immediate relief is often the first response that pops into their minds. The donors know they have far more resources than the people in need. Relief is fast, relatively easy, and doesn't require a long-term commitment from the provider. Once we have sent a container of food to a community hit by a natural disaster, we can sleep well, feeling good about ourselves. We've saved lives and helped solve an emergency problem—at least temporarily.

Another reason why development isn't implemented more often is because it's very difficult to reverse the dependency created by the relief systems that are currently operating. These systems are embedded in organizations and ministries that exist primarily, or exclusively, to deliver relief.

But when people in need become dependent on donated relief, they are hindered from entering into the abundant life that God intends for them. Stifled in their growth, they often lack trusted local leaders who are equipped to invest the time and energy needed to disciple them and help them grow in all aspects of their lives.

For the relief providers, the feeling that comes from having people depend on them and appreciate what they do is very addictive. We all like being thanked, admired, and respected. It can be difficult for people in the spotlight to want to share their skills, because by doing so they risk no longer being needed or sought after. But though it may seem unnatural, it's a godly impulse to want to teach others the skills we have mastered, to empower them to do the same things we can do, to help them attain self-sufficiency so they no longer have to depend on us or anyone else (except God, of course).

Relief workers, teachers, doctors, and other professionals are not intentionally oppressing the poor; but by hoarding their skills, they perpetuate an upper-class/lower-class system. Nobody would admit to that, and they are probably unaware that it's happening, but reinforcing class distinctions is the exact opposite of what Jesus did. He discipled those closest to him and gave them authority. He told his disciples that they would do even greater works than he had done.[3] Can you imagine how difficult it must have been for the Son of God to place that kind of trust in a ragtag group of sinful humans?

Is It Ever Good to Give Relief?

Relief is a viable option in the days immediately after a disaster or emergency, when lives are at stake and basic systems are broken. In severe cases, we *must* provide relief, or else there won't be any lives remaining to undertake the process of development.

Relief is often a necessary short-term solution as part of a broader crisis management program. But even when relief is justified, the best practice is to distribute it in partnership with local churches, so that it can be established from the get-go as a missional activity rather than a purely humanitarian operation.

Partnering with the Local Church

After identifying the active churches in a community, we can bring the pastors together and ask them, "How do you think we can respond to this crisis in a God-honoring way?" and "As we quickly respond to this emergency, how will we know when it's time to move on from distributing relief?" and "What needs in the community should we plan to address after the initial crisis has passed?" The local churches and their pastors can then take the lead role throughout the relief process and guide the transition into development efforts. If the church is seen taking responsibility for the needs of the community, the people will take notice. God's wholistic mission on earth thereby gains respect and grows in stature in the eyes of the community.

Unfortunately, too often it doesn't work that way. Typically it's more like this: A ministry organization becomes aware of an emergency and immediately ships food and/or supplies to the affected community. Along with staff and volunteers from outside the affected region, their teams arrive and start handing things out—with a camera crew recording it for the organization's social media feeds.

Then, when supplies run out or the emergency situation is no longer in the news, the teams pack up and leave. No lasting connections have been established in the community, and no partnerships have been formed with the local churches. Who do the people now turn to for help in rebuilding? Where do they find solace or comfort, or answers to their questions about why this happened to them? If you represent a Christian organization but you do not partner with the local churches, you are actually undermining the leadership of the local pastors and working against the influence of the church in that community. Relief without development, and riding to the rescue rather than partnering with the local church, are damaging on so many levels. It's a sad reality, but this is what happens when we rush in with all our resources and try to solve problems quickly, rather than serving, equipping, empowering—and *allowing*—the local church to be the heroes so that God ultimately receives the glory.

Begin with the End in Mind

In Haiti, when a powerful earthquake destroyed much of Port-au-Prince and the surrounding towns and villages, countless buildings were reduced to rubble. The infrastructure of the nation was in ruins. Obviously, emergency relief was needed because more than one million people were suddenly homeless. People's lives were in grave danger. They immediately needed drinkable water, sanitation, and food—the basics of life. That is good and necessary relief, which must be provided without delay. But if an organization is still providing relief two or three years after the earthquake (as happened in Haiti), they're no longer doing relief work, they're doing the people a disservice.

Early in the relief phase, it is good to discuss with your local church partners when to begin transitioning to transformational development activities. Equipping the people to rebuild their lives and their homes is a big step toward empowering them to live on their own with dignity and self-respect.

Prolonged relief can stifle any progress you might otherwise make toward development. Local recipients of the relief will say, "Why should I get dirty and use my hands to work and grow crops when I can go line up and get a box of free food?" Instead of working to become self-sufficient, most people, when they realize they don't have to go to the trouble of planting, weeding, and harvesting a crop in order to eat, will just sit back, do nothing, and wait for the next delivery. Relief is addictive, and it can destroy development.

Consider what it does to the recipients to continue receiving handouts—it takes away the joy and satisfaction of self-sufficiency. It dehumanizes them by stealing their dignity, undermining their confidence, and belittling them as they begin to perceive themselves as incapable of meeting their family's needs.

If we continue providing relief when development is the better response, we can do far more harm than good. Loving "the least of these," as Jesus would have us do, requires that we prayerfully consider how God would have us treat our neighbors. We must ask the question, "Would I want to be treated like that?" We need to seek ways to help the underprivileged experience the abundant life that God desires for them, and discover the local resources he has already provided in their own community to allow them to get back on their feet and meet their own needs.

When a Bandage Is Not Enough

Because only a small fraction of the poverty in the world today is a direct result of a natural disaster or other emergency crisis, simply mounting a huge relief campaign and delivering tons of donated goods to the poor isn't going to bring an end to global poverty, or even to localized poverty. What is needed is not a bandage on the wound, but a total healing.

This is why a sustainable model of transformational development—inseparably linked with the local indigenous church to bring about a wholistic solution—is the only real hope for lifting people out of the seemingly endless cycle of poverty that has spanned lifetimes and generations.

Secular relief agencies can't do it—they're incapable of doing much more than saving physical lives. The church, as God's representative on earth, is the only institution that can effectively bring lasting wholistic transformation to heal the physical, spiritual, and psychological brokenness that holds so much of the world in bondage.

Look at the stark differences between relief and transformational development:

	Relief	Transformational Development
When Appropriate	Disaster or life-and-death situations	Improving normal daily life
Duration	Short-term	Long-term
Resources	Import resources from outside the area	Maximize the use of local resources
Ownership	Outsiders	Local people
Required Situation	Emergency, to save lives	Normal life, leading to self-sufficiency
End Result	Possible dependency or exhaustion	Sustainability and independence
Type of Action	Reactive, curative, done for people	Enabling people, proactive prevention
Relationship	Only transactional	Relationships with impact

How would you feel if somebody came into your town and looked at you with pity rather than respect? What if they came to your house and ignored you but gave your children toys and something to eat? And what if those strangers came back the next day and fed the kids again, and did it every day for a week—and then went away and you never saw them again?

Your children would look at you, hungry again, waiting for food you don't have. To make matters worse, the group that brought relief never helped you learn how to give your children food on an ongoing basis; they simply created dependence. That's meddling and interference, not love.

What Can We Do about It?

It comes down to each one of us examining the ways we express love to our neighbors. We're not saying it isn't godly or right to feed a community that is truly in need. Jesus identifies with the poor and commends us for serving them: "I was hungry and you gave me food, I was thirsty and you gave me drink. . . . Truly, I say to you, as you did it to one of the least of these my brothers, you did it to me."[4]

But that isn't the entirety of good news for people living in poverty. The abundant life Jesus came to give isn't limited to a meal, something to drink, clothes, and a visit. It's inviting people to be transformed in every area of their lives and helping them achieve it. As you feed them today, what are you doing to empower them to be able to feed themselves tomorrow? And as you develop their capacity to provide for their own physical needs, what are you doing to meet their need for spiritual nourishment?

When you decide to engage in the work of development, you cannot go into it thinking that people's lives and their communities will change immediately. Development is a long-term process of gradual, sustainable change. Though a catastrophic event may have brought their needs to the forefront, the people you're seeking to help did not fall into their current situation overnight. By the same token, the deep-seated problems they face are not easily fixed and will not be resolved quickly.

A Healthy Perspective on Transformation

As you begin the process of helping people move toward transformation, it's helpful to remember that there are probably some areas of your own life still in need of development. You may not be wondering where your next meal is coming from, but you also may not be living the fully abundant life that God intends for us. Just as the people you're trying to help need to be transformed, there are also areas in your own life that still need God's work of transformation.

When this truth sinks in, you'll be able to help others with dignity, humility, and respect. Realizing that you still don't have it all together will help you rely less on your own strength and resources and more on God's power and provision.

Finally, clothed in that humility and prepared to stay the course for the long term, you need to ensure that the work of development is not something you are doing *for* the poor, but instead, it's a journey you're undertaking *with* them. Those who are going through the process of transformational development must be fully involved, increasing their knowledge and skills, and becoming empowered to provide a better, healthier life for their families.

God intends for people, communities, and entire cultures to be transformed to reflect his goodness and glory. Society is changed as individuals undergo change. Nations are discipled as people are discipled.

Development takes longer than relief, and if you're radically changing directions, expect times of discouragement and occasional failure. People have been held in the bondage of poverty, racism, and violence, and there are no instantaneous solutions to these deep-seated problems. It's easier to give food for a day and then walk away than to help people obtain their own food and find freedom, self-sufficiency, and a new outlook on the future.

Disciple-making is part of the work of transformational development. When enough people in a community have experienced that transformation, it reaches a critical mass, and then like ripples in a lake, it continues to expand, affecting the lives and communities around them.

If it seems easy . . . then it's probably *not* transformational development!

Questions for Reflection and Journaling

1. How has your understanding of *relief* and *development* changed after reading this chapter?

2. What have you seen modeled in the ministries you've observed—relief, development, or both? Describe your observations.

3. Thinking back to the analogy at the beginning of this chapter, what are some of the forces that create the "holes" people fall into? What would it look like to fill in those holes or prevent them from being dug in the first place?

12

SHORT-TERM MISSIONS IN PARTNERSHIP

A hammer can be a good tool or a bad tool, it depends on how it's used. So, too, it is with short-term missions.

LARRY RAGAN

Let no one seek his own good, but the good of his neighbor.

1 CORINTHIANS 10:24

FLORENCE

Taylor, a senior in high school, is excited about joining her church youth group on a short-term missions trip to Guatemala during spring break. She is taking classes to deepen her understanding of God's love for people throughout the world, and to avoid cultural faux pas. As she prepares for a week of service among the needy people of Central America, she's looking forward to working on a painting project and spending time with the local children. The cost of the trip is something she can't afford on her own, so she's been asking extended family members and friends to help provide the money she needs to pay for her airfare and other expenses. She is also asking people to pray for her and the rest of the team.

The Lasting Impact of Short-Term Missions (STMs)

Like Taylor, a lot of people get their first taste of world missions on a short-term trip. For many, it's valuable exposure and a life-changing experience.

We've known young people like Annie, who decided to go into missions full-time after experiencing her first short-term trip to the Middle East. We know professionals like Norm, at the peak of his career as a lawyer, who realized during a short-term missions trip that he was called to give his prime earning years to God's work internationally. There are so many more—like David, a leading cardiologist, who returned from a short-term trip with a new personal mission: "We need to do this in my city!" And Claire, who is currently working in full-time missions in a very difficult nation because of her experience on a short-term missions trip to Afghanistan.

Still, for many, the question remains: Is the value of STM trips primarily for the people who go? Or can the work done on a short-term trip also have lasting value for the people served?

It's easy for people from affluent societies to return from a short-term missions trip buzzing from the experience of going somewhere exotic and charged up with a sense of accomplishment because they gave relief items to some very impoverished people. But were any lives actually changed?

One of the main criticisms of STM trips is that they provide minimally effective poverty relief to communities whose real need is long-term development. For that reason and many others, some churches have stopped sending short-term missions teams at all, not wanting to waste time and money, and out of fear that they might actually do more harm than good.

While Charlie and I were discussing some of the unintended outcomes of short-term missions trips, he spoke one simple sentence that put the value of STMs in perspective: "I wouldn't be sitting here today if I hadn't gone on short-term missions." Even with a problematic missions model, good work can be accomplished, and lives—of team members and people in the host community—can be transformed. Charlie has witnessed and experienced both firsthand.

On his very first short-term missions trip, Charlie's group visited Ms. Lena, who lived in a tiny shack in Jamaica. After knocking at her door a long time and getting no response, they were let in by one of the local leaders. Ms. Lena was lying in bed, too weak to get up, but when she saw the group, she began singing hymns, and the group started worshiping along with her. When Charlie asked how she got her food with no social programs to help her, she said, "Oh, it's simple. When I need something, I pray—and God sends a neighbor or someone like you." That lesson of completely depending on God was something Charlie learned on his first missions trip, and he has never forgotten it.

Where STMs Go Wrong

Many people would point to Haiti as a prime example of the failure of short-term missions. American churches have been sending STM teams to this impoverished nation for *decades*, and yet it's hard to see any lasting results from their efforts—especially considering the large financial investment all these trips have required.

That's not to say that STM teams waste their time. They typically are busy doing lots of things. Sometimes they spend long days doing exhausting work, but too often it's not something that has a lasting impact. It's sad when groups travel to a place of great need and *do* and *do* and *do* and *do*, and yet no transformation results from all their doing. This happens, in part, because so many short-term missions trips are standalone projects, not part of a strategic development plan designed to transform the community and its people.

Two Waves of the Developmental Tide

Transformational development doesn't happen *to* a community. It must happen *with* a trusted local partner in the community. When a partnership is formed between a local church and an outside missions organization or sending church, the initiative begins with training a group of leaders in the principles of wholistic transformational development (WTD). An essential part of this important first step is helping the participants identify the resources and capacity they already have in their community. They learn that dependence on outside assistance undermines their ability to take ownership of their development process and lay the necessary groundwork for lasting change.

This is the *first wave*—the essential foundational training during which the community and local church determine their priority needs and set up a framework to undertake an initial development project (which we call a *seed project*). During this early stage of training, inviting STM teams to visit the community is highly discouraged—we

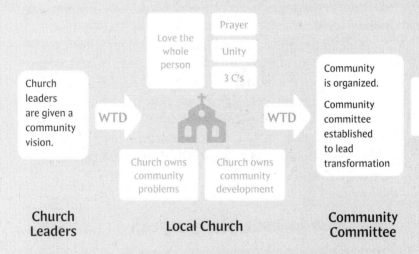

FIRST WAVE
Foundational Training

Love the whole person

Prayer

Unity

3 C's

Church leaders are given a community vision.

WTD

Church owns community problems

Church owns community development

WTD

Community is organized.

Community committee established to lead transformation

Church Leaders

Local Church

Community Committee

don't want to cause confusion about accepting short-term outside help or reopen the wounds of dependency.

Once a long-term strategy is in place and the local leaders have begun to see success from the seed project, they will have a better understanding of how their cross-cultural partner can help with specific training and assistance.

That's when the *second wave* can begin—inviting select short-term teams with specific skill sets to empower the community to solve existing problems or increase the capacity of the local community to sustain the work on their own. These could include ministries that equip the community by training, or ministries that support the implementation of projects such as water drilling.

Targeted STM visits can help the local churches establish their

SECOND WAVE
Empowerment

Identify and address felt needs

Like-minded outside organizations are invited to participate in empowerment projects to meet the felt needs of the community.

Local Community

relevance in the community and demonstrate their ability to serve their neighbors. But without the indigenous local church taking the lead, and unless the short-term teams have been taught how to work effectively with their local partners, a short-term visit could undermine the fragile development process before it even gets off the ground.

Components of Successful STMs

We believe that God has given every community the resources they need to experience the abundant life he intends. That's why, very early on, those being trained to work in the community must be able to identify the many resources they already have.

Long-term partnerships

An average American walking into a Haitian community might see *zero* resources—and typically that lack of vision would be communicated to the locals: "Wow, look at this poor place! There's nothing here to work with!" But a person from another developing country entering that same Haitian community would probably notice lots of resources that the American would miss. That's why it's important not to bring anyone or anything into the community during the first wave that would undermine the foundational work that is underway.

Working together cross-culturally allows each partner's strengths to cover the other's weaknesses and enriches both the ministry experience and the outcome. The process of building an effective long-term partnership takes transparency, intimacy, trust—and, of course, time. The more time you can spend with your partner organization, and the more you increase your exposure to their culture and to the people in their community, the more easily you will be able to identify both resources and real needs.

For example, along with an American supporting partner, I spent a week in Jamaica, visiting the ongoing Life In Abundance work there. During a walk through the community, we happened to see a group of ladies being taught how to quilt. The American partner mentioned that her church also had a women's group that met weekly to do quilting. That coincidental, unplanned exposure to an ongoing development program opened the door for these two churches to connect in a meaningful way. The Jamaicans had already determined to become self-sufficient and use the resources they had in their community, so it was perfect timing for teams of skilled quilters from the American church to visit Jamaica on short-term missions trips to help the local ladies increase their skills. This equipped the Jamaican women to create better quilts, which increased the value of their work and allowed them to better provide for their families. The connections and relationships built by that kind of cooperative activity proved to be very beneficial to the ongoing development work in that community.

A cooperative working relationship designed to address real needs identified by the local partner produces two important ancillary benefits (in addition to the value of the actual work). First, it allows the visiting partner to confer honor and respect to the local partner. This, in turn, authenticates and validates the work of the local partner in the eyes of their community. In many cases, it elevates the status of the local partner to have a confident, skilled team of outsiders visit. People in the community notice! When short-term teams subsequently share a positive testimony and leave behind something of value, it gives honor to the local church and shows the community that the church is important enough to have the active participation of helpful foreigners. And that testimony ripples out.

Planning, effort, trust, and communication

Short-term missions teams can be structured to do considerable good—but they require prior training, a shared vision, participation in the field, end-of-visit debriefs, and active follow-up.

Most important, they must be consistent, and they must contribute to an ongoing program, not just take on a random project designed to fill the visiting team's schedule and help them feel good about their trip.

Increased exposure between partners to each other's work and community, along with time spent together, exposes new opportunities to find and utilize each other's existing resources. Part of an indigenous partner's responsibility is identifying the resources available in the community and clearly communicating those to the outside partner. So if an outside partner says they want to send in a short-term team to provide a certain type of assistance, the local pastor could reply, "We appreciate your help, but let's discuss some other needs, because we believe our local community can handle that one on our own."

When undertaking transformational development, the visiting partner must never do something for the indigenous community that they are able to do for themselves with their own resources. Stepping in would rob them of their self-worth and confidence in their own abilities—mindsets that are necessary for long-term self-sustainability. If a partnership is built on trust, and there's an open and honest flow of communication, the local partner must feel free to say, "No, we don't need that right now." And from there they can redirect the help to something they *do* need. We cannot over-emphasize the importance of local control and direction of the transformational development process—which must be firmly rooted in trust and open communication.

Without trust and communication, the senders are left to decide what they think is needed, and then they go ahead and do it—regardless of how necessary or helpful it might actually be. The effectiveness of short-term missions is determined by the health of the long-term partnership. Unfortunately, it doesn't always work out the way it should.

The missions pastor of a large church with a generous missions budget might call a partner ministry in the field and say, "We want to send some short-term teams this summer. What can we do for you?" The local partner might respond, "Okay, send us the dates," and then start scrambling to find things for the visiting teams to do. The local partner may be thinking, *We have to maintain our facility and pay the staff salaries, so we need to keep these teams happy to make sure their church continues to support our ministry.* And so they find ways to keep the teams busy, to satisfy their need for ministry gratification; and they send the teams home happy, feeling as if they've made a difference.

But that's not a transformational partnership; it's a transactional arrangement. And it does nothing to build long-term, sustainable development.

Focusing on a singular goal

Both partners need to share the same goal: the enduring transformation of a community and its people. All outside assistance must be evaluated for its strategic effectiveness. A short-term missions team may be there for a week, but the year has fifty-one other weeks as well. What happens then? Has the short-term team helped to create something viable and sustainable, or did they just work on a one-off project that could have been done better—and more economically— by local people in the community? Were the short-term missionaries part of a strategic plan, building on work that is important to the transformation of the community? Or were they just a distraction?

Short-term missions visits are a great opportunity for the team and the indigenous church to disciple each other. For example, when a church youth group wants to take a short-term missions trip, the local church leader could respond by saying, "We also have a bunch of young people in our church, and it would be great if these two groups could work together on a particular outreach we've been praying about." That way, they can learn from each other. The receiving church and local community are both enriched, and the youth group from the sending church returns home having grown through their experience of ministering cross-culturally with others who are also undergoing transformation. They will have done actual ministry and left behind lasting fruit in the community.

But here's the thing: The outreach (or whatever it might be) must be generated by the local indigenous church as part of their transformational development and ministry, not something the short-term team does for a week in lieu of painting a building.

Local ministry partners need to know they have the freedom and confidence to discuss with the short-term teams how best to work together as equal partners. Partnerships driven by love build lasting friendships and long-term results that bring honor to God. When all partners value each other and recognize their equal status, equal identity, equally valid perspectives, and equal empowerment, good things happen.

Short-Term Teams Can Produce Unexpected Results

CHARLIE

I have led many short-term dentistry teams that visited partnering churches with the goal of training pastors from that region how to do basic emergency dentistry. During the visit, we treat some people from the local community to allow the pastors to learn how to correctly diagnose the problems that produce serious pain in these patients. But our primary goal is to replicate ourselves as practitioners.

As the trained pastors become more proficient and confident, they begin to share their skills with other leaders, training them to do the same work in other communities.

Some of the benefits we've seen could not even be imagined when we first began the training. In India, for example, after we had trained some of the local pastors in dentistry, one village pastor was riding home on his motorcycle and accidentally hit a young boy. The residents of the town were outraged and ready to carry out some street justice.

When the chief of police arrived at the scene, he recognized the pastor as the dentist who had treated his mother, saving her from the constant throbbing of a painful toothache. To the police chief, this pastor was a celebrity, a man of great stature, someone deserving honor and not the anger of the mob. So the police chief intervened with the angry townspeople and calmed the situation—all because the pastor's new skill in dentistry earned him status and respect.

Clear, Honest Communication Is Vital

We've learned that churches need to think much more broadly about the resources they have that might be useful to their ministry partners. For example, Southeast Christian Church has sent teams to work with women's ministries and leadership training. Those resources could have been overlooked as unnecessary; but when those needs were identified by the partners, the resources ended up being of great importance and great impact.

We also need to think about how to offer resources, though this can often happen naturally as partners converse and ask questions. We might say, "Hey, have you heard of this special training that would equip your team to do this or that? If it's something that would be of value, we could facilitate it for you, if you'd like." That's much better than saying, "Hey, we've recruited a skilled team to come to your site and train you on this topic." The receiving partner must feel the freedom and have the authority to say, "Yes, I think that would be so helpful," or "No, we don't need that, but let me tell you what we really need instead."

SECC's missions department created what we call a *toolbox*—a list of ideas, resources, and areas of expertise found within our church community, many of which can be provided by a skilled short-term missions team. Once we've progressed to a certain level of strategic planning with a local ministry partner, we invite them to browse through the toolbox. Some items include training in innovative ways to raise funds; leadership development seminars; training in how to work with volunteers; medical screening clinics—so many diverse offerings. But it's up to the partner to say, "That particular item in the toolbox is just what we need. Can you provide it?"

Indigenous partners can also participate in giving what *they* have. An overseas partner might look at a large American church and assume they have so many resources that they could not possibly have need of anything. But we all need *something*. Remember the apostle Paul's analogy of the body of Christ and the human body in 1 Corinthians 12:12-27. Any one church is just one part of the body—and the body needs all parts working together in order to function as God intends. In short, *we need each other*.

Every local church is incomplete. It has needs that another part can provide. It is important that we all have this mindset: Every local church has resources to *share*, and every local church has resources they *need*—though it may not always be clear to a local body what they need to receive. That's true for every church around the world, regardless of size.

Some churches have an obvious need for certain resources, but they may not be as quick to recognize the skills, experience, and insights they can share with their partners. Likewise, some churches (typically Western "sending" churches with established missions programs) have obvious skills, experience, and insights to share with their partners, but they may not be as quick to recognize their *own* needs, and what they can *receive* from their partners.

I have noticed that when my American church friends spend time with their brothers and sisters from LIA, ministering alongside one another, they see things they would not experience living in the United States. For example, when faced with the overwhelming poverty they find in some parts of the world where we send teams, they realize that all their material resources are completely inadequate and they must rethink their approach. This rethinking leads to a deeper dependence on God and a greater commitment to prayer—which they witness firsthand in the lives of our indigenous friends.

The Western approach to missions tends to be one- or two-dimensional. But when we partner with local indigenous churches, we see the complexity of the situation and the high value of relational ministry.

Working within a Western model of ministry, we have a tendency as Americans to *read* Matthew 25 and *do* Matthew 25—that is, give food, water, clothing, and shelter—and then stop there, rather than asking the next-level question: "Why are you without food, water, clothing, or shelter in the first place? What is the root cause of your lack?" Indigenous partners have been forced to address these needs without the material wealth most American enjoy, and they can help us see that there is a better way to respond, a way that truly glorifies God.

Indigenous church partners can help us see the shortcomings of our short-term missions efforts and teach us how to make those efforts more fruitful and relevant. (The local church members are good coaches, if we will let them.) Moreover, where Western missions groups can get locked into relief ministry and not know how to move forward into development ministry, our indigenous partners can model effective ways to transition from relief to development—again, if we will let them.

Some of the training our American churches have received from LIA include the practice of prayer, approaches to inner healing, understanding spiritual warfare, building relational ministries, experiencing the presence of God, living with an eternal perspective, learning freedom in worship, and embracing community.

Benefits of a Great Short-Term Missions Team

With the Life In Abundance headquarters in Kenya and ministry offices in thirteen other nations, we have been on the hosting end for many short-term teams. We are thrilled at some of the benefits that typically accompany the arrival of an STM team. They have tremendous energy, they bring enthusiasm, they are an encouragement to the local churches, they're problem-solvers—just to name a few. And those are benefits they may not realize they bring with them.

Well-prepared short-term teams that come with a clear purpose and well-trained local churches that understand how the visiting teams fit into the overall development strategy are a dynamic combination. They are partners in the truest sense—empowering the locals, imparting valuable skills, and increasing the capacity of the local churches to serve their communities. Dynamic STM teams bring answers and resources to meet what the local church has identified as a critical need. And when the teams leave, they take with them the unique gifts that the local church has imparted to them in return. When it works that way, that is true partnership, and it's what gives short-term missions a valuable role in transformational development.

Questions for Reflection and Journaling

1. What was the most successful short-term missions trip you've been involved with—either as a goer, prayer partner, or supporter? What made it successful—for you as well as for the people served?

2. How has this chapter affected your perspective on short-term missions?

3. Describe the next short-term missions trip you hope to be involved with (or your first, if you've never gone) and how you will do it appropriately and well.

13

DON'T SEEK THE GLORY

A man may do an immense deal of good,
if he does not care who gets the credit for it.
JESUIT FR. WILLIAM STRICKLAND

For from him and through him and to him are all things.
To him be glory forever.
ROMANS 11:36

FLORENCE

Mud huts and grass roofs were all we could see in this small village in northern Ghana. Two missionaries, Francis and Pamela, had been trained by Life In Abundance in Kenya and were implementing the biblical model of wholistic ministry in that region of West Africa.

The church in that village had been growing so steadily that they had outgrown their older concrete block building. It was no longer able to hold all of the people coming to Christ!

One day as Francis and Pamela were visiting the pastor, he said to them, "I've seen you around with some white people. Could you ask them to come and build us a new church?"

"Why would I do that," Francis replied, "when you and the people here are capable of building your own church?"

Francis reminded the pastor of the resources he already had

in his community: Sand, cement, and other raw materials were inexpensive, and there were many masons and carpenters in the church. Francis also coached the church leaders on how to plan and execute a capital campaign. Together they discussed the need for a larger building in light of the biblical principles of wholistic ministry and the importance of self-sufficiency. The pastor and other church leaders knew that through their training in transformational development, they had been empowered to take ownership of their own long-term change; so they agreed to undertake the building project themselves without foreign involvement.

At about the same time, Francis and Pamela helped the church members learn how to farm more efficiently and harvest larger yields. (A short-term team from the USA was invited to help train the church in farming skills appropriate for their region of the world.) The farmers also discovered they could buy their seed in bulk as a group and save money. As their earnings grew, they were able to increase their giving to the church.

The men of the church decided they would donate their time and labor every Saturday to make the concrete blocks needed to construct the new church building. We were there visiting Francis and Pamela during that time and saw stacks of more than ten thousand blocks the church members had made in preparation for the construction. With stamina and determination, the church soon completed their new five-hundred-person building. They converted the old church building into a preschool run by the church to benefit the community.

When other churches in the region saw the new building that this congregation had funded and built themselves, they asked to be taught how to do the same thing—and the training in transformational development multiplied into these new communities!

God was already at work. All the church leaders and people had to do was to get involved with what God was blessing. God has given the church his Word to instruct and guide us, and the Holy Spirit to empower the church to be the agent of transformation for the community he loves. And all of this is for his glory.

If somehow this pastor had connected with a church in the West to construct a new building, they probably would have found a group willing to both pay for it and send a series of short-term missions teams to build it. Instead, the project was completed with no outside funds or labor. The members of the local church did all the work, and God received all the glory—rather than a Western partner riding in and riding out as the hero.

Thank You So Much!

"Thank you" is one of the first phrases most of us learn when traveling to another country. Not only is it a polite response when we are given a cup of tea or welcomed into a home, but it usually brings a broad smile to the faces of the people we're thanking. Why? Because we all like to be appreciated. It just feels good.

In fact, it feels so good that it can actually become addictive.

During my time in Ethiopia more than twenty years ago, after three years of hard work in that local community, I had become well known, a household name, admired and respected for what I was doing. I was happy to be seen as the hero; I thought it validated the results we were seeing, and it also felt good—that is, until I realized how powerless I really was. I couldn't even throw a Christmas party for the hundreds of poor children living so close to us on the garbage dump.

It was hard for me to come to the realization that I needed help—that I couldn't do it alone, and that I needed to stop trying to be the savior for that community.

God Loves Unity among His People

I finally understood that God had been at work in that community in Ethiopia *long* before my family and I ever showed up as missionaries. Thus, my role was not to determine what needed to be done and then try to do it on my own; rather, it was to prayerfully seek God's wisdom and direction to get a sense of what he was *already* doing, so I could join him in his work. When we align ourselves with God's perfect plan—the ongoing work that he has started and will bring to completion—it becomes obvious that we are not heroes riding to the rescue. God is the one who makes all things new, and that's why all the glory belongs to him.

Still, so often it seems easier to go it alone—we're in control, we work in familiar and reliable ways, and we know our objectives, so we can choose the easiest way to accomplish them. Mobilizing other people, sharing a vision for ownership, and accommodating others' opinions and ways of working can be cumbersome, inconvenient, and even frustrating. Inviting input, feedback, critique, and correction from those we serve or partner with can make us feel vulnerable and uncomfortable, especially if we were already thinking we could accomplish the tasks better without their contribution. The easier path is to assume leadership and instruct others to follow what *we* think is the best course of action.

Bringing the Heroic Impulse Back Down to Earth

CHARLIE

Taking charge, leading, and going for the glory—that's how we've been taught to get things done in the West. So many of our contemporary stories and movies are built on the actions of superheroes—the ordinary person who suddenly becomes larger than life and saves the day. We dream of the adulation that comes from taking the last-second shot and winning the game, risking it all and snatching victory from the jaws of defeat. But it's not just the winning we crave; it's also the roar of the crowd and the fame that accompanies the triumph.

That same warmhearted feeling infuses donors when they give money to help save lives and support humanitarian organizations that continue providing aid—sometimes far past the time when relief activities are necessary or even helpful, as we've mentioned. We've seen time and again that people would much rather donate toward emergency relief efforts than give to ongoing development work. Relief is such an easy sell. The donor immediately receives the satisfaction of writing a check, sponsoring a child, or providing meals. It feels good to do good—and that's not bad. It *should* feel good. The problem is when we start believing that writing a check or providing immediate relief does anything to solve the recipients' long-term needs. Or when our donations make us feel praiseworthy or heroic.

There are countless problems in the world that could use the services of a powerful superhero. Hunger, poverty, disease, slavery, injustice, dirty water, war, and no access to education—all of these are symptoms of a broken and fallen world. Like Florence and me, many people have felt drawn to enter those quagmires to work toward solutions and bring healing to the victims.

With all good intentions, we tried it on our own, and that lasted for a few years until we saw how truly enormous the problems of poverty and poor dental health really were. And we realized we could not be the heroes anymore.

The Pathway to Transformation

When people are truly transformed and every aspect of their lives begins to change, other people take notice and start talking about it. The news spreads quickly. Soon others want to discover what happened so they can experience these changes in their own lives and families. It doesn't take many changed lives to initiate the transformation of a community.

Transformation can start with relief—"I was hungry and you fed me"—but God's mission on earth doesn't end with feeding people. We must lead them to God, which means we must address the chains of injustice and other issues that hold people back. We must bring them to a point where they can be fully discipled. Then they will be equipped and motivated to go back to their communities and their neighbors and walk with them through the process of sustainable transformation.

The problems come when we see a situation of need and want to go fix it right now. Maybe it's to correct an injustice or address an apparent problem of provision. Maybe it's just to show other people that we're doing something. But let's not forget that God sees the same injustice or problem, but with infinitely more depth and clarity. He also sees the mask that conceals the pride or insecurities that are propelling us to *do something*. Rather than rushing in with our own devices, wouldn't it make more sense to ask God to show us the approach that *he* desires? How can we respond so that all the glory goes to God?

Though some relief workers might not admit it (apart from in a weak, exhausted moment), it's possible they'd rather not see the recipients of aid rise to become their equals—to have the same skills, abilities, and opportunities as the foreign humanitarians. Often they don't seem to have a heartfelt desire to see the locals as valuable participants, much less partners. It makes for better job security to continue helping and feeding people, rather than equipping them to become self-sufficient. Perhaps the worst thing a relief worker could hear is, "Thanks, but we don't need you any longer."

I hope no one would intentionally keep another human being from becoming independent, and most relief providers will assure you that doesn't happen; but their actions suggest otherwise. To local onlookers, it can seem as if the relief workers don't want to share their skills—because if they did, they wouldn't be as needed, as sought after, or as valued as when they first arrived as the heroes.

Looking Beyond Our Own Abilities

FLORENCE

If you go to another country as a missionary and you have teaching skills, for instance, you naturally want to flourish in your role as a teacher, and you want the locals to want to be your students. They look up to you with admiration because you are trained in the West and you have degrees and so much knowledge to share. It's understandable that you would see yourself as the best one for the job and that your calling is to apply your skills, experience, and expertise *directly*—that is, by teaching the students yourself rather than investing your time developing local teachers to do what you do. It's not that you're trying to hold people back or take the glory for yourself, but maybe you've never thought about what's possible in terms of long-term development, sustainability, and impact.

Let's imagine you believe that God wants you to become a missionary. You pray and ask him to lead you into the best way to fulfill his agenda for you as a missionary. Perhaps you then sense an affinity for medicine and decide to study to become a missionary doctor. As doors begin to open in that direction, it's easy to lock in on a preconceived notion of how you will fulfill God's mission in your life. Maybe as the path unfolds before you, you don't pray as much about the specifics. Once you are well on your way to becoming a doctor, maybe you become less willing to ask God, "What do *you* want me to do?" because you have already spent considerable time and money preparing to be a doctor. That's who you are now.

The point is that no matter how much training, experience, or knowledge we might have, we never outgrow or outpace our need for continual dependence on God to lead us in the details of our lives. The danger is that we begin to lean on our own understanding and stop actively trusting God to make our paths straight.[1]

So if you take what you've been trained to do, and you believe that by doing it you are faithfully serving God and extending his mission, but you don't continue to seek God faithfully and daily for his wisdom and direction, take heed. It doesn't take too great a stretch of the imagination to think that your work might be creating an unhealthy dependence on yourself and your skills, like the missionaries I observed in my hometown while growing up in Kenya, or like Charlie before he started training others to do as much of the dental work as possible.

Again, the point is not to lean on your skills and experience but to submit them to Christ, allowing them to serve *his* purposes rather than your own. It is understanding that we are ambassadors of Christ before we are accomplished professionals.

That's why I wanted to pursue ordination: to be branded as a servant of Christ rather than just as a medical professional and to be sure that I would serve from that posture, giving the glory to Christ and not seeking it myself. The day I surrendered all to God and allowed him to own me, I dethroned myself and enthroned Christ so I would follow him without question.

We're Created to Give Glory to God

Jesus taught us in the Sermon on the Mount, "Let your light shine before others, so that they may see your good works and give glory to your Father who is in heaven."[2] It is okay for people to see your good work and acknowledge that you did well. If you have done it as a servant of Christ, although they appreciate your work, they will give God the glory because it is clear that he is the one you are serving.

Our base, human, innate desire is to be appreciated, needed, and thanked. In our natural human state, we seek to be the hero, to receive recognition and glory. But as Christians, we are no longer bound to our natural human state. That old self has been put to death and buried. Our new self no longer seeks to be honored, but rather to reflect all honor and glory to God, the Creator and Lord of the universe.

Scripture tells us that we were created to glorify God, to reflect his glory and to proclaim it to all creation.[3] Our lives, our desires, and everything we say and do are all to be given for one reason—to give glory to God. He yearns to bless us as we follow him and extend his Kingdom, but as the prophet Isaiah tells us, God is jealous of his glory, and he will share his glory with no one.[4]

Psalm 96:3 invites us, "Declare his glory among the nations, his marvelous works among all the peoples!"

It is God who must receive the glory, and all nations are called to declare it. It is his glory, not ours, that he expects us to declare.

Questions for Reflection and Journaling

1. Describe a time when you felt special, like a hero or a VIP.

2. What would it take in that situation to give the glory to God, instead of enjoying it yourself?

3. In what ways does your life bring glory to God right now? And how would you like to increase that?

4. What is the role you play in the body of the global church?

14

PROGRAM OWNERSHIP BY THE LOCAL CHURCH

*Jesus is the hope of the world, and the local church
is the vehicle of expressing that hope to the world.*

ANDY STANLEY

I will build my church, and the gates of hell shall not prevail against it.

MATTHEW 16:18

FLORENCE

Heavy rain had been falling for days, and my husband, Festus, and I were driving past the impoverished community of Mekanisa, Ethiopia, headed back to our house after attending language school. As we drove through the pouring rain, I noticed someone walking along the road. It was our friend Tadesse, a young man who had repeatedly invited us to visit his small village church.

He waved for us to stop, and as he climbed into our car, soaking wet, he invited us to take the opportunity right now to visit his church.

We thought, *Well, how can we say no?* So we agreed to go.

Tadesse pointed the way down a terribly rutted dirt road littered with deep potholes—now filled with rainwater and mud—that severely challenged the capabilities of our pickup truck. Both sides of the road were lined with houses—shacks, really, made with scavenged wood, plastic, sticks, and mud. These were tiny dwellings, measuring on average ten by ten feet. Little children, filthy, poorly dressed, and with no shoes, ran back and forth across the street in front of our truck. Others stood by their houses, while still others played in the pools of dirty rainwater alongside the road. Piles of smelly trash littered the soggy landscape.

Upon our arrival at the Mekanisa church, I immediately regretted our decision to come. I knew that my first step out of the truck would result in my foot and shoe sinking deep into the mud. From previous experience, I knew this particular "black cotton" mud would quickly adhere to my shoe like thick, wet concrete. Despite my reluctance to even step out of the truck, it was too late to turn back. We had come this far, and we were committed.

Festus and I managed to navigate the quagmire, and once inside the church, we met the pastor and were given a short history of the congregation. They had started meeting two years ago, initially as a fellowship in a mission compound; but the mission had closed, and the church moved to this rented building. About twenty-five church members gathered every Sunday morning for worship. Concerned about their poor community, this tiny congregation had already started to help by undertaking a project to sponsor children from the homes surrounding the church building.

As we concluded our visit with prayer and were getting ready to leave, I heard a voice behind me say, "You will come back to this church and preach the Word from this pulpit."

I turned around, thinking it was my friend Tadesse playing a joke on me, only to realize there was no one behind me. I was bewildered. I had definitely heard a voice speak to me very clearly. Then a wave of panic washed over me as I realized that God must be telling me I would minister in partnership with this church. That was a frightening thought because it did not align with my future ministry plans *at all.*

I took comfort in the fact that I was only halfway through my course at the language school, so no ministry here would likely happen for quite some time. Still, the thought wouldn't leave my mind. Every time I drove past this community on the highway, its misery and its many physical needs called out to me, and I knew I had to do something to help.

At the end of that year was the Christmas Eve when I invited the local children to our home for Vacation Bible School—the story I shared in chapter 5. As you may recall, I knew there was no way I could manage four hundred kids by myself, so I approached the pastor of the church in Mekanisa, meekly asking for help. Ten people from that tiny congregation volunteered, and with their help the Christmas party was a marvelous success.

After all the children had left and the cleanup was finished, the church volunteers joined me for a short time of worship and prayer. We enjoyed our time together, and they committed to help start a regular Bible study. This led to a second Bible study, and by the summer I was leading four Bible studies each week, specifically for people living in the slum community.

Then came a request from Agidew, the church's pastor. Knowing that I was a medical doctor, he asked if I could do a health screening for the children they were serving through their outreach project. How could I say no after they had so generously helped me with the Christmas Eve party? I recruited another missionary doctor, and together we gave medical examinations to all the children in the community. It wasn't until after those screenings that God began to reveal the solution to the great needs of the community.

We discovered that 85 percent of the 320 children we examined had an active disease. The five top problems were worm infestations, skin diseases, eye infections, respiratory infections, and AIDS-related illnesses. And 60 percent of the children screened positive for more than one active disease. Though we gave everyone medicine for these problems, it was likely that, given their existing living conditions, close to 100 percent would revert to the same medical status within three months. On top of that, I knew that the spiritual health of their families was even more critical.

After performing hundreds of health screenings and compiling the findings, I couldn't just walk away and hope that someone else would step into the void and work to improve the health of this community. But I also wasn't exactly sure what to do. From my experience in similar settings, it was obvious that relief efforts were not the answer. This wasn't an emergency situation or a response to a disaster. I knew they needed something more, something truly transformative that would bring about lasting change.

I prayed fervently about the problems I had seen firsthand. I asked God for *his* solution, and he answered me. I recognized that the problem was bigger than any one person could handle, and I was coming to understand that the local church was God's choice to be the change agent in the community. When I met with the church leaders to present the data from the health screening, I also proposed that we partner together, using a wholistic approach, to change the overall health status of their community. They agreed, and our cross-cultural medical ministry was born.

The church chose eight people for me to train in how to implement the necessary changes. They became my very first team. After ten days of training, using a curriculum I developed based on materials from the African Medical and Research Foundation, as well as the book *Multiplying Light and Truth through Community Health Evangelism* by Stan Rowland, we were equipped to start. That initial curriculum has since been updated many times; but it's still being used, and it's still working!

Following the training team graduation, and after a time of prayer and fasting, their first activity was to invite the community members—especially those with children—to come to the church and discuss the findings of the health screening. They came by the hundreds. The eight team members explained what had been found during the medical screenings and what had been identified as the root causes of the children's health problems.

While this meeting was taking place, I stayed home to pray. Remembering the missionaries I grew up with, I wanted to be certain that I, the outside expert, wouldn't be seen in a leadership role. It was important for the people to see the trained team members as the leaders in their community, not me. And the leaders needed to be heard in the context of the local church's presence in the community.

The team emphasized that medicine was not the solution to the community's health problems. And they made it clear that the community as a whole was responsible for ensuring the health of all its residents. The meeting ended with a charged and committed community wanting to see change. They chose nine committee members, half of whom were church members, to create a plan for making the community a healthier place. The community selected the nine because they were already respected and known as people who could be trusted.

The next activity was to train the new committee members on issues of development, health, community organizing, and transformation strategies. After completing this training, they were empowered and fully convinced that they now had the answer for transforming their community. They called the people together to choose health promoters—one for every ten households. The church also chose spiritual health promoters, paired up with those chosen by the community, to evaluate the spiritual health of the families during home visits, and to start the work of evangelism.

We organized the community into nine clusters, each led by a committee member working with a training team member. Each cluster had between thirty and forty families, with a health promoter and a spiritual health promoter for every ten families. These clusters met once every two weeks in the church building to plan and implement health development initiatives. During these biweekly meetings, they also watched part of the *JESUS* film and discussed it as a group.[1]

The clusters took it upon themselves to clean public toilets, clear drains, repair the houses of those with leprosy, and gather and burn trash. The enterprising spirit of these cluster groups was amazing!

Moreover, all the activity was community-based and church-led. The health promoters and spiritual health promoters started home visits, bringing prayer and health education into each home. Quickly, the community's behavior began to change.

Next, the teams surveyed every household to identify and prioritize needs. We learned that more families than we had initially realized were fully dependent on begging as their only source of income. In response, we helped the committee apply for a grant from an outside church aid agency that could teach basic principles for starting an income-generating activity or business and start a revolving loan project for micro-entrepreneurship.

After a year of community mobilizing and organizing, we noticed that many of the men were stepping back—not participating in training or income generation and leaving the responsibilities to the women. To address this, we planned a dinner event—for men only—with a well-known speaker. We sent invitations to the men, and thankfully they came. The teaching highlighted the importance of their role as men, and the speaker warned them that if they didn't take up their position and lead the community, their wives would step into the vacuum and take on those roles. That woke them up!

These programs, and many others, were created to address the root causes of the felt needs in the community. By the three-year mark, here are just some of the programs the church and committee had implemented:

- Vocational training in carpentry for the men and tailoring for the women. The community clusters selected candidates to benefit from learning these skills.
- A church-based kindergarten, teaching both children from the middle class (who paid fees) and children from among the very poor (who got a free education and a daily midmorning snack).
- A microenterprise program, helping many people in the community start small businesses.

- A sports ministry involving the youth of the community.
- A new child sponsorship project.
- A church-based library and tutoring services to promote literacy.
- House and kitchen renovations for the very poor, especially the homes of leprosy patients.
- An HIV/AIDS ministry with ten trained "care and support" providers, headed by a nurse who was also a local church member.

During those same three years, inroads were made with the community, and trusting relationships developed in a once violent and seemingly hopeless situation. Rowdy and disruptive gang members came to the Lord. And short-term teams from the US came to work in the community, alongside church members and missionaries from our agency.

Meanwhile, the church had grown from 25 to 350 adult members, with 500 children participating weekly in the Sunday school program. Not only that, but the church had also planted several daughter churches in the region. The church members had grown spiritually, and some (including my friend Tadesse) were pursuing a seminary education. The church's times of worship had deepened and become vibrant. The prayer and intercession ministry was steady and powerful, with continuous, ongoing prayer—even during church services.

The church continued to sponsor medical camps—either hosting them or working in partnership with other groups—to address both the physical and spiritual needs of the community. The most obvious change after three years was in the community's health indicators. Health screenings continued as a monitoring tool—initially every six months and later yearly—and the percentage of those who were sick steadily declined, despite an increase in HIV/AIDS in the community.

At the end of the third year, we started to phase out from hands-on participation in this community, and by the end of year four, our direct involvement had ceased. But the local church has continued the work, and we are now mutually regarded as peers in God's work.

I should also mention that this was the first project funded by a partnership of our organization with Southeast Christian Church. The program supported us for $600 per month, which totaled $21,600 for the three-year duration. Now compare that with what it would have cost to send a missionary doctor's family from America to serve in Ethiopia. I share this information because the donors need to know the return on their investment. In this case, you have read about the many positive outcomes produced by this initial project—including a transformed local church, changed lives and families, improvements in health and well-being under very difficult circumstances, and the metamorphosis of a community.

We know from repeated visits back to this church that they have now birthed other churches, and they've trained those new churches in the principles of transformational development. That once-tiny church has now started a nonprofit organization, registered with the government, so they can undertake additional development projects in other parts of Addis Ababa. So by any measure, the work of this church in its surrounding community has produced a great return on the investment entrusted to it.

If you visited this church today, you wouldn't hear about the great work that Life In Abundance did or that Southeast Christian Church made possible. Our names would not be mentioned. Instead, you would hear about the many ways in which the local church took the lead in the development of their community. All the honor and glory would go to God and to his bride, the local church—and we rejoice!

We left behind a self-sufficient, motivated, growing, and empowered church that is multiplying sustainable community projects. We were joyful about a newly mobilized and organized community, owning and participating in their own developmental needs and advocating for change with a unified voice. This community has benefited greatly from healthy collaboration with outside partners. And through those partnerships, they have developed and implemented many new initiatives that in turn have produced sustainable transformation.

Local Transformation Brings About Global Impact

The Mekanisa community spread the news that, by working together, change is possible! Before long, we were involved with two other community-based interventions through local churches in Addis Ababa, and the word soon traveled to other churches in Ethiopia, both urban and rural, as well. With the registration of our new organization, Life In Abundance, in 2012, the work quickly spread to eleven other countries in Africa and two in the Caribbean. All praise be to God!

As local churches take leadership and ownership positions in the development of their communities, many benefits, such as the following, can be seen:

- Development becomes a God-sized venture owned from within the community.
- The church becomes self-propagating, because the testimonies of transformed lives can easily be seen, and those stories draw people to the church.
- People are radically changed for the long term and equipped to bring about change in others.
- The church becomes a community resource. This enables the outside partners to move on to help others, while the local church continues to build on the foundation the partnership has established together. The ongoing work is sustained by the church and the local community, not by outside intervention.
- Cross-cultural missions becomes participatory and reaps the benefits of integrated ministry: sustainability, empowerment, and phaseout.

- Most important, it empowers and builds confidence in the local church, which becomes, in a glorious way, the institution that Christ intended. This transformation has nothing to do with our leadership or our programs—in case we might be tempted to take the credit and boast about it.

To God's glory, we have seen this scenario repeated over and over again. I could tell similar stories of a church in the slums of Cairo, local churches among the displaced in South Sudan, and many, many more.

Paradigm-Shaping Principles

In the course of our first three-year initiative, we learned vital operating principles that have helped us partner with local churches in cross-cultural missions ever since. All these principles were modeled by Jesus during his earthly ministry:

- He went about as a discipler, to empower and train.
- He used the community-established structures of communication and accountability.
- He showed care and concern for the whole person.
- He relied on discernment and intercessory prayer.
- He proclaimed the gospel and alleviated people's urgent needs—for food, healing, and protection.

The results of his ministry included real and sustained changes in people's behavior. His solutions to problems were innovative; interventions were established to become examples that could be replicated; and to those in power, a voice was raised for the poor to be served with respect and dignity.

Through the years, we've learned a lot about partnering with local churches, and we've been surprised by some of the vital lessons God has taught us. Local churches in the marginalized and poor areas where missionaries are likely to serve are usually humble in structure and small in numbers. Pastors often have to work full-time, doing something other than church work, in order to support their families. Leadership tends to suffer from lack of rest, low motivation, and lack of growth in the church. Their Sunday services are disorganized, and—probably most shocking of all—the congregation seems to be just fine with all their problems; they don't seem agitated at all!

When we first entered the Mekanisa community, we could clearly see that the local church had been right smack in the middle of a very needy community for a long time; and yet we didn't see much evidence that it had made any difference at all. There seemed to be little strategic planning and very few programs in place to bring about change in the community.

We had no desire to step in and try to lead the church. In fact, we were afraid they would slow us down or pull us into projects that were outside our scope of ministry, that they would keep us from fulfilling what we saw as our calling. As it turned out, of course, we were quite mistaken.

God's plan was best.

Jesus Christ is the hope of the world, and he founded the Church; so it shouldn't come as any surprise that his plan to bring transformation to communities is through the work of the local church—the community of believers that God chooses to bless. Without the collective and organizing power of the church, and the blessing that God attaches to it, the ability of Christian workers to have an impact on the world is greatly compromised.

The local church is God's vehicle to express hope to the world; and its function rests primarily in the hands of its leaders, no matter how unqualified they may seem. Cross-cultural missions can reap the benefits of integrated ministry, sustainability, empowerment, and phaseout. But the key is the local church, the bride of Christ, the institution that Jesus promised will prevail.

Questions for Reflection and Journaling

1. When did you first realize that the church is not a building where people gather? How is your local church currently involved in a wider ministry outside its walls?

2. What does it look like for a church to have a strong wholistic ministry?

3. What are some practical ways that you can allow other people to receive the credit for work you've helped accomplish?

4. How has this chapter opened your eyes to the importance of working through the local church? What is the Lord saying to you in this regard? Spend time listening to the Spirit to see how these ideas translate to your context.

15

DISCIPLES MAKING DISCIPLES

The greatest issue facing the world today, with all its heartbreaking
needs, is whether those who, by profession or culture, are identified as
"Christians" will become disciples—*students, apprentices, practitioners—*
of Jesus Christ, *steadily learning from him how to live the life of the*
Kingdom of the Heavens into every corner of human existence.

DALLAS WILLARD

A disciple is not above his teacher, but everyone
when he is fully trained will be like his teacher.

LUKE 6:40

FLORENCE

When we prayed alongside that flowing river during our first visit
to Haiti, we realized that God was clearly leading us to enter that
community and begin the work of transformational development. I
picked up some stones from the riverbank and took them home with
me, like a proxy or point of contact with Haiti.

Realizing that Life In Abundance would need to send trainers
to live among the Haitians, I approached a Kenyan couple, Dorcas
and George, about taking on a new disciple-making mission. When
I told them, "I believe God is calling you to Haiti," they believed it
too, and I gave them the rocks from the Haitian river. Throughout
their time of transition and preparation to go, those stones were on
their desks, reminding them of the people and the land they would
soon be joining in ministry.

The Haitian pastors invited Life In Abundance to conduct a seminar with every interested church leader in their community to help them envision how it could be transformed and what would be needed. We introduced the pastors to wholistic ministry and examined the vital role of the local church in that transformation. The church leaders realized there was a stark difference between what we were proposing and the relief programs in which they had previously participated. Together they talked about the importance of churches taking ownership of their community's development and integrating their congregations as leaders and trainers in serving the vulnerable and the poor. Together they talked about dependency and the vast difference between relief and development.

At the end of the first day of this vision seminar, we asked the pastors and church leaders to examine their hearts to see whether God was leading them to be part of this very different approach. If they felt that this plan was from God and was what their community needed, they were invited to return the next day to complete the seminar.

On the second day, more than half the pastors did not return. We have found that this is normal, and we are not discouraged. We know there are any number of reasons for people not to come back. The kind of work needed to bring about lasting change is not for everyone. And really, we only want those who feel called by God to be in the partnership. We don't want to be unequally yoked with someone who doesn't buy in to the model God has given to seek true transformational development.

At the end of the second day of the vision seminar, we shared this story:

> Three friends need to cross a river. One of them has done this several times before and knows the path that's safe to walk and how to negotiate the currents and irregular riverbed. He decides to guide the others across, one at a time.
>
> As they are making their way, the inexperienced friend becomes afraid. He is very unsure of his footing. Because

DISCIPLES MAKING DISCIPLES

he cannot swim, he fears he might slip beneath the surface and drown. He refuses to take another step and wants to be carried. So the leader picks him up and carries him to the shore of a small island in the middle of the river.

The leader rests for a moment and then says, "Okay, I'm going back to get our other friend, and I'll return for you."

So the friend who has experience crossing the river goes to get the other friend and says, "I'm tired from carrying that guy, and I don't have the energy to carry you. If I do, we might both be in danger; but don't worry—I'll teach you how to cross the river safely under your own power."

They start wading in the water, and they're making good time crossing the river. The leader is giving instructions, and the friend is doing as he is directed, step-by-step. They are going along so well that they forget to stop at the island, and instead they keep walking toward the other shore.

The poor guy left on the island sees them passing by and yells out, "Hey, come get me! Help me!"

The friends in the river call back, assuring him that he can make it—if he will just get in the water and follow them. But he is afraid and refuses.

The two friends in the river continue safely to the other side, as the one who is stranded on the island keeps calling out for help, finally realizing the sad truth that he has been abandoned.

After telling this story, we asked the remaining pastors some questions.

"Have you ever had someone promise to take you to a destination, but then leave you stranded partway?"

The pastors were almost angry as they answered, "Of course. Many people have done this to us. They need to come back, keep their promise, and finish what they started."

So we asked, "Whose problem is it really? Could it be your

problem? Perhaps you have not allowed yourself to be taught; maybe you stopped making progress, waiting instead for someone to come and carry you to the next place . . ."

We saw the light bulbs going on around the room as they began to see the moral of the story.

We told the assembled church leaders that we were neither going to carry them *nor* abandon them, but we were willing to teach them and work with them for three years so that they could learn to teach others and be empowered as members of the local church, the bride of Christ, to take their rightful place of leadership in the community.

Finally, all that remained was to ask, "What do you believe is God's plan for Haiti, and what is his desired future for this community? What is God saying to you? What are you sensing? As leaders in this community, what do you believe God has for your people?"

As they spoke of their hopes and dreams for their community, a group who caught the vision came together and became encouraged and excited to take the next step. This core leadership group asked LIA to come to Haiti and partner with them to see their community transformed in a way that could be sustained for years to come.

By the end of that vision seminar, they said, "Yes, we are on board. We are ready. What do we do next?"

We responded, "Okay, we will ask a trained Kenyan couple to come live with you for three years and disciple you in these things. And by the end of the three years, you'll be fully able to continue this work on your own."

They wanted to start as soon as possible, so Dorcas and George moved to Haiti and began to further develop the relationships with these churches. What they saw when they got to Haiti would have discouraged most people, but Dorcas and George were no strangers to extreme poverty, and they saw the hope and promise of what these villages could become. They planned the initial Training of Trainers sessions and chose the team that would be trained.

Development Success in a Relief Quagmire

The core group of pastors agreed to partner with LIA for three years. With the constant presence of Dorcas and George, the Haitian churches successfully implemented an initial seed project with an investment from LIA. Once that project was completed and proven to be successful, they began working on a strategic list of projects that the church leaders and townspeople identified as most needed. With help and resources from Southeast Christian Church, initial projects were undertaken. After the work of transformational development had gained solid traction, SECC and other churches could send many short-term teams to help in specific areas of need, as identified by the Haitian church leaders. And when the three-year term ended, Dorcas and George went home to Kenya. Their work was done. The local churches were able to sustain and grow the programs they had started, and God received the glory. Today, no one in that region of Haiti knows the name of the ministry that discipled them—and we couldn't be happier! It's not about us. The hero is the local church.

Though Dorcas and George were willing to leave their home in Kenya and live in Haiti for three years—modeling prayer, conducting training, and continually discipling the local churches—today it is rare for LIA to send outside leaders into a community to spearhead the development efforts. Normally, we identify a trusted and respected local leader, whom we disciple, train, and equip to be the local representative. A local team is then assembled to work with this leader. Together they train and disciple cohorts from churches throughout the region.

This same process we used in Haiti has been repeated in multiple cultures and nations around the world—even in affluent countries such as the United States.

Long-Lasting Fruit

I returned to Haiti after many years and rejoiced to see what God has brought forth—the beauty of it! The transformation has continued, and the results are incredible. The local churches that were part of the initial program have multiplied the number of trainers and have taken these principles to surrounding towns. Now there is a Haitian country director and a Haitian doctor working at a clinic set up by the local churches. The people have been transformed, and the effects are seen in every area of their lives. They have permanently moved from dependence on outside assistance to sustainable self-sufficiency. A trained indigenous team is on hand, helping churches that initially struggled to find their footing. It's amazing to hear these churches talking about how they are helping other churches and communities—sounding as if they have always done things that way!

Transformational Development as Disciple-Making

The process of transformational development is actually a disciple-making process. But for many Christians, when they read the biblical passages, discipleship doesn't sound all that appealing:

> Whoever loves son or daughter more than me is not worthy of me.
> MATTHEW 10:37

> If anyone would come after me, let him deny himself and take up his cross daily and follow me.
> LUKE 9:23

> Sell your possessions, and give to the needy.
> LUKE 12:33

> Whoever does not bear his own cross and come after me cannot be my disciple.
> LUKE 14:27

Any one of you who does not renounce all that he has
cannot be my disciple.
LUKE 14:33

I chose you out of the world, therefore the world hates you.
JOHN 15:19

Those who belong to Christ Jesus have crucified the flesh
with its passions and desires.
GALATIANS 5:24

I have suffered the loss of all things and count them as
rubbish, in order that I may gain Christ.
PHILIPPIANS 3:8

Unfortunately, many people who call themselves Christians seem
to view discipleship as an optional deep dive into following Jesus, sort
of like a graduate course for truly holy believers. Sadly, that is not the
case. Following Jesus means going all-in, holding nothing back—as
many of the verses above make abundantly clear. Either we are disciples or we must seriously question our faith.

In stark contrast to our modern practice, the New Testament
equates discipleship with being a Christian. When referencing followers of Christ, the New Testament uses the term *disciple* 269 times, and
the term *Christian* only three times.[1] True followers of Christ know
that becoming like Jesus is the goal, and discipleship is the biblical
means of learning his ways and growing to be like him.

Today we have multiple ways of transferring information, of
teaching and learning—including traditional in-person schools,
online courses, intensive weekend seminars, and millions of books
and study guides—but that isn't how things were done in the first
century when Jesus was teaching his first disciples.

In the time of Christ, if you wanted to learn a skill, you would apprentice yourself to someone who was an expert in that discipline. You would do any task they asked of you, no matter how trivial or menial it might seem, in order to gain the teacher's trust so that they would have confidence in you as a worthy receiver of their knowledge and skills.

Jesus called twelve men to leave their lives and livelihoods to follow him and become his disciples. His teaching pedagogy was highly relational and wholistic. He did far more than simply dictate information. He modeled a practical illustration of the truths he taught. The disciples followed him, listened to what he said, watched what he did, and asked questions. In this way, his values were imprinted on their hearts and minds. Then, when Jesus gave them an assignment or sent them off in teams to minister on their own, his disciples knew what to do because they had seen it successfully demonstrated multiple times by their mentor.

Wholistic Discipleship

Just as Jesus' discipleship method was wholistic, so was the subject matter he covered. He was concerned for the entire person— everything that concerned them and their lives was a concern to him.

Oddly, when Christian leaders talk about the Great Commission today, they often focus on the first section, "Go therefore and make disciples of all nations, baptizing them in the name of the Father and of the Son and of the Holy Spirit," and the last section, "And behold, I am with you always, to the end of the age," while often ignoring the middle section, "teaching them to observe all that I have commanded you."[2] But that middle section is where the wholistic part of disciple-making happens.

Jesus often taught about the issues of life that modern discipleship programs seldom address. He taught about psychological issues: anger, anxiety, and holding grudges. He was concerned with relationship issues: integrity, revenge, love, marriage, lust, hate, and forgiveness.

He addressed social issues: injustice, refugees, taxation, debt, and imprisonment. Physical needs were a constant concern of his: hunger, thirst, blindness, leprosy, incurable illnesses, and even death.

In short, Jesus demonstrated his love and concern for the whole person. His final recorded words to his disciples during his earthly ministry instructed them to disciple others as he had discipled them—wholistically, caring for the whole person.

Churches today tend to focus only on the biblical training aspect of discipleship, often ignoring huge issues running rampant in the lives of the congregation. And we have some big issues!

Though the divorce rate among committed Christians is lower than that of the secular world, it still affects far too many families in the church.

Pornography and other sexual issues are rampant among clergy and congregants alike.

We don't love our neighbors, and we don't particularly like a lot of the people we spend time with on Sunday mornings.

And those are just a few examples.

It's time we faced the facts: The world has problems, yes, but we have plenty of our own!

Just as impoverished communities in the developing world need to experience wholistic transformation, the Western church needs it as well. Otherwise, how will the world know that Jesus is worth following?

Our *Being* Must Inform Our *Doing*

Scripture tells us, "The Word became flesh and dwelt among us."[3] The Word is Christ himself. He came into the world so that we might have life—abundant and wholistic life.[4] That life is the result of our *being with* him, instead of simply *doing for* him. We enter that abundant life when we, like his first-century disciples, spend time with Jesus and imitate him.

It's the *being with* that breathes life into the strategy of our *doing*. Anyone can pick a strategy and implement it, but if it doesn't come from seeking God in prayer with a surrendered heart; if it doesn't connect us with the local church—the body of Christ on earth— then it will not be a life-giving strategy. Two people—one seeking the heart of God, one not—could implement the exact same plan; but the first one will be life-giving, while the other will be dry and lifeless, with no lasting impact. For us to be able to bring life to the places where we serve, it's not just about reading God's Word, internalizing it, and allowing it to breathe life into us and into our work—though studying and internalizing Scripture is certainly central to our lives. It's just as much about seeking the wisdom and guidance of the living God for the *specific situations* in which we find ourselves. It is the power of God that breaks the yoke of bondage; and unless we are abiding in him so that his power can move through us, the bondage will remain.

Partners Submitting One to Another

When we talk about disciple-making in the context of a cross-cultural partnership, we have in mind a *mutual mentoring* relationship. By this we mean both partners—the typical "sending" partner and "receiving" partner—submitting to one another, showing genuine *mutual* respect and expressing an openness and willingness to learn from one another. Each partner can be both mentor *and* student, depending on the situation. We must recognize that neither partner has all the answers. In humility, we must be open to receive wisdom and insight from our partners. This two-way mentorship, or coaching, is the catalyst behind this new wave of missions. As we determine not to seek admiration and respect for ourselves, we must be intentional about being open to receive from our partners, as together we serve those to whom we have been called.

"As iron sharpens iron, so one person sharpens another."[5] In these trust-based relationships, we submit to one another, sharing what we have, what we know, and what we have experienced. As we nurture this kind of partnership, it creates an atmosphere that energizes our ministries and mission activities. Jesus equipped his disciples and released them to do the work of disciple-making. As modern-day disciples following in the footsteps of our Lord and Savior, we are to do the same. Jesus is the ultimate discipler. We are his disciples, and he has commissioned us to make new disciples wherever we go.

Cross-Cultural Discipleship in the Same City

CHARLIE

Adopting this principle and engaging in disciple-making with an international partner has greatly affected Southeast Christian Church and the wider Christian community in Louisville.

We recognized the wide gulf between the suburban churches and the urban churches in our city, and we knew this disconnect didn't glorify God. We had a great hope and desire to bridge that gap and partner with our brothers and sisters in reaching our city with the gospel of Jesus Christ. We had tried many times over the years to heal the rift and build trust and have fellowship together, but nothing ever seemed to work. Every attempt had failed. Generations of distrust, fueled by misunderstandings, broken promises, and actions that seemed unloving and uncaring had left scars that resisted healing. Then SECC asked Life In Abundance if they would be willing to send a staff member from their office in Kenya to join our church staff in Kentucky to lead disciple-making work and train our team in how to partner cross-culturally, using wholistic transformation development.

LIA agreed, and a senior leader and trainer joined the Louisville staff. He wasn't seen as a guest; he was accepted as an integral part of our team—one of us. He used the biblical principles of wholistic ministry as the core of his teaching. In the places where LIA works, they call it Training of Trainers, but in the American context we decided to call it Equipping for Community Transformation. As our people began learning the principles we've been teaching in this book, we began to see changes in people's attitudes and perspectives.

Our team began to see the importance of partners in ministry receiving from each other—that ministry isn't a one-way street. And that's true whether our cross-cultural partner is in Africa or just across town. Whatever the factors are that separate our cultures, we can learn from each other, and we can help each other grow—if we will trust each other in Christ's love.

As a result, we started praying against the strongholds of racism, unforgiveness, bondage, and distrust in our city. We prayed to experience the unity in the body of Christ that Jesus prayed for—and it made all the difference in the world.

As we opened our arms again to the urban Black churches, we began a conversation that demonstrated our sincerity and our desire to learn from them. When, with humility, we expressed our desire to minister together as equals, the entire situation began to change. The urban churches realized we were not looking down on them because they lacked some resources that we might have; but instead, that we saw their strengths and recognized ways that we could be a blessing to each other. A whole new partnership began—one that proved to be very valuable, especially when Louisville was again rocked by racial violence and injustice. We were able to come together as brothers and sisters in Christ and show our city what it looks like for Black and white church leaders to speak against injustice and call for reconciliation with a united voice. This collaboration was possible only because of the mutual disciple-making we had engaged in and the foundation of trust that was being built and strengthened as a result.

In discipling, we model and teach a deeper love for and obedience to Christ. Attempting to disciple others apart from that overflowing love may look virtuous, even heroic, but it will eventually wear thin and run out. If we try to disciple without love for the whole person, we may help some people look like Christians and overcome a degree of poverty, but they will lack what they need most: new hearts filled with real affection and devotion for God and their neighbors.

Theologian R. C. Sproul described discipleship well:

The pursuit of God is not a part-time, weekend exercise. If it is, chances are you will experience a part-time, weekend freedom. Abiding requires a kind of staying power. The pursuit is relentless. It hungers and thirsts. It pants as the deer after the mountain brook. It takes the kingdom by storm. . . .

It is a pursuit of passion. Indifference will not do. To abide in the Word is to hang on tenaciously. A weak grip will soon slip away. Discipleship requires staying power. We sign up for the duration. We do not graduate until heaven.[6]

Discipleship is nonnegotiable, and disciple-making is a command for all Christians in the Great Commission. Many Christians look for confirmation in a "calling," but Jesus didn't call his followers to his mission; he called them to himself and then commissioned them to go out into the world. If you're walking with Jesus, the terms of the Great Commission are incumbent upon you. Faithful disciples must become faithful disciple-makers.

Go therefore and make disciples.

Questions for Reflection and Journaling

1. What does *disciple-making* mean to you?

2. How have you been mentored by someone who encouraged you and shared their experience, skills, and knowledge with you?

3. How are you discipling others right now?

16

COLLABORATING
IN UNITY

*The unity of Christendom is not a luxury but a necessity. The
world will go limping until Christ's prayer that all may be one is
answered. We must have unity, not at all costs, but at all risks.*
BISHOP CHARLES HENRY BRENT

*Behold, how good and pleasant it is when brothers dwell in unity! . . .
For there the LORD has commanded the blessing, life forevermore.*
PSALM 133:1, 3

CHARLIE

"There is no indigenous Christian church in that nation," a group of
medical missionaries told me when I met them at the Global Missions
Health Conference (GMHC) in Louisville.

Hearing this, my heart sank. I can best describe it as agony. I had
recently returned from that same country. I had been in the churches
and worshiped with the local people, and I knew there was a thriving
indigenous church, though they had to meet in secret.

No doubt this group of medical missionaries had done great service in that country for the twenty-five years they had focused on
improving health conditions there—and doing so in Jesus' name.
But they were surprised to hear that I had personal experience in
that country, and they were shocked when I told them I had been

working with the rapidly growing underground church. Though they had worked in this small closed country for decades, they had no idea that any local church existed there.

The GMHC has facilitated many connections between missionaries and organizations that were otherwise unaware of the other's existence. Thousands of people from around the world attend this annual gathering for the opportunity it affords to network and learn together.

Southeast Christian Church and Life In Abundance felt that the same kind of gathering should be replicated in Africa, to meet the growing demand for strategic networking and teaching in the Global South (the traditionally poorer regions in South America, Africa, and Asia).

So Global Missions Health Conference–Africa was launched in Nairobi as a partnership between Southeast Christian Church, Life In Abundance, and the Christian Medical and Dental Association of Kenya. The goal was to meet an immense need for shared learning and connection for those working tirelessly to affect global health and missions across the continent; and to wholistically equip Christian professionals, missionaries, students, and church leaders to inspire transformation in their individual areas of expertise.

After several years of successful gatherings, GMHC–Africa broadened its focus to become the Global Missions Conference–Africa, creating a platform where attendees can share their missions experiences and learn from one another. This conference has fostered unity in the body of Christ among like-minded Christians as they grow to better understand sustainable transformational development and the importance of unified partnerships in their work for the Kingdom— because none of us can, or should, do it alone!

The Importance of Working in Unity

Unity is a key principle that is close to our hearts, as we've learned the importance of working together in spite of our many differences—endeavoring to see lasting transformation come to the people and communities we serve.

For Florence and me, ministry has evolved and grown over the years. And because we come from very different backgrounds and perspectives, we've had to learn to appreciate the value of listening to each other and benefit from the varied experiences that God has sent our way.

Throughout Paul's letters to the early Christian churches, he continually emphasizes unity. In his message to the Philippians, he speaks of "being of the same mind."[1] Paul isn't saying that we all must share the same opinions. "Being of the same mind" means being united in our beliefs, thinking along the same lines, in a way completely shaped by our common commitment to Jesus Christ. Our witness to the world depends on our demonstrating love for each other and showing that—despite our varied backgrounds and perspectives—we can come together as a rich and vibrant body of believers, in unity, harmony, and one accord. The unity of the Spirit is something the world cannot fathom.

As Paul writes in 1 Corinthians 12:4-6, "There are varieties of gifts, but the same Spirit; and there are varieties of service, but the same Lord; and there are varieties of activities, but it is the same God who empowers them all in everyone."

Describing the church as a physical body, Paul writes:

If the foot should say, "Because I am not a hand, I do not belong to the body," that would not make it any less a part of the body. And if the ear should say, "Because I am not an eye, I do not belong to the body," that would not make it any less a part of the body. If the whole body were an eye, where would be the sense of hearing? If the whole body were an ear, where would be the sense of smell? But as it is, God arranged the members in the body, each one of them, as he chose. If all were a single member, where would the body be? . . .

The eye cannot say to the hand, "I have no need of you," nor again the head to the feet, "I have no need of you." On the contrary, the parts of the body that seem to be weaker are indispensable, and on those parts of the body that we think less honorable we bestow the greater honor. . . . God has so composed the body, giving greater honor to the part that lacked it, that there may be no division in the body, but that the members may have the same care for one another.[2]

Unity Despite Differing Strategies

We may disagree on the specifics of how to accomplish our missions objectives. Some organizations mainly provide relief and others work for long-term sustainable development. But the two approaches can work together, as long as they are part of an overall strategy that emphasizes local capacity, local direction, local empowerment, and sustainability, and if the organizations involved are willing to submit to one another.

In our experience, we've seen that it's possible for relief organizations to work effectively with development organizations. For instance, a well-known relief agency approached Southeast Christian Church to partner in a missions program in which members would package family-size portions of soup mix and fill up a forty-foot shipping container with about thirty tons of emergency food to send as relief. One of the SECC pastors had heard about the program being done successfully elsewhere and really loved the idea. He told the other pastors, "We've got to do this at SECC!"

I was in a meeting with my missions team, who knew the dangers of creating dependence through ill-advised relief efforts. I said, "Here's a new program that Southeast is partnering in. We're going to pack four containers of emergency food, and—"

Before I could even finish the explanation, my team said, "No, forget it. We can't do that."

I said, "Yeah, we're going to pack a million meals, four containers full—but don't worry. I've already called Florence, and Life In Abundance is going to work with the relief agency. They're going to figure it out together. So let's get our church people ready to pack the meals."

At that time, Life In Abundance knew that a partner church in Uganda was experiencing a huge wave of refugees entering their region. There was a real need for emergency food for a limited time, and then the refugees would need other kinds of development assistance. In a wonderful spirit of unity, Life In Abundance joined hands with the relief organization to help the Ugandan church meet the immediate need of hungry refugees in a significant way.

Once the emergency was taken care of, LIA quickly moved into working with the local church to help the community start the process of sustainable transformational development.

Packing the meals was an enriching experience for the members of Southeast Christian Church. It bonded people together and got them thinking more about missions. At the same time, SECC launched a program for members to fund community development for a period of three years. Because it had a predetermined end date, the support would not create dependence, and it helped the community that received the food initiate ongoing programs to bring lasting change.

It was a great lesson for our missions team and me to experience— that we could join with other types of organizations without compromising our core beliefs and principles. And LIA learned that relief could be leveraged through the local church for significant impact without creating dependency.

Unity That God Desires and Blesses

Unity is such an important characteristic of the body of Christ that, on the night he was betrayed, Jesus asked his Father to grant him that his followers would be unified. John 17:20-21 records his prayer—which encompasses our generation as well:

> I do not ask for these only, but also for those who will believe in me through their word, that they may all be one, just as you, Father, are in me, and I in you, that they also may be in us, so that the world may believe that you have sent me.

Unity was important to Jesus because he had seen how his followers could quarrel; and he knew that, left to their own devices, it would be rare for them to ever get along. But if they were clearly united—"being of the same mind, maintaining the same love, united in spirit, intent on one purpose"[3]—it would be so unusual that the world couldn't help but notice.

King David gives us another insight on unity in Psalm 133:

> Behold, how good and pleasant it is
>> when brothers dwell in unity!
> It is like the precious oil on the head,
>> running down on the beard,
> on the beard of Aaron,
>> running down on the collar of his robes!
> It is like the dew of Hermon,
>> which falls on the mountains of Zion!
> For there the LORD has commanded the blessing,
>> life forevermore.

Psalm 133 celebrates the beauty of God's people dwelling together in "good and pleasant" unity. We have all experienced times of disunity, and the antonyms *bad* and *unpleasant* would be apt descriptors.

The second verse refers to the anointing of Aaron as Israel's first high priest. The oil flowing from the crown of his head down onto his robe symbolizes the blessings of God flowing onto the people.

The third verse speaks of the water that comes to the mountains and flows down to the people, refreshing the land and quenching thirst. Then the psalm concludes, declaring that God so values unity that where it exists, he commands a blessing. And when God commands something, you can be sure it comes to pass.

If you and I want to experience the anointing, refreshing, and blessing of God, we must seek to be in unity with one another and work to establish and maintain that unity.

Disunity Hurts Global Missions

I have fished extensively throughout North America, and on many occasions I've seen eagles soaring and hunting. Eagles are top-of-the-food-chain predators, and they're not known for working in cohesive teams. When a bald eagle shows up, the other birds back away. The eagle is here—taking over and in charge. And the other birds get the leftovers.

The bald eagle symbolizes how missions have too often been done in the past. We Westerners fly in with our money, ideas, and power. We're accustomed to being in charge and getting things done quickly. There's little sense of sharing or equality. We fly in and take over the airspace. It's bad and unpleasant. It's human nature, as well as animal nature—but it's not God's nature. We need to see the value in pursuing unity and receiving God's blessing.

Western organizations are accustomed to taking leadership and fixing things. They bring their resources to bear. But I've learned—by working with Florence and LIA—that recipients of the traditional top-down model of missions are left dealing with the repercussions of this approach. By applying biblical principles that are not prioritized in the Western church and are more in line with African culture, LIA has been able to experience tremendous fruitfulness where Western organizations have struggled to see fruit. Being discipled by LIA has been a tremendous blessing for Southeast Christian Church and has shaped how we do ministry in our own community. At SECC, we've learned a lot through the eyes of our African brothers and sisters about how to approach needy people with dignity, and how to work in concert with local churches, even in communities where they are not yet respected or effective in meeting people's needs.

How do we see Jesus' prayer for the unity of his disciples come to fruition in our lives and ministries? How do we experience the "good and pleasant" unity that David speaks of? How do we develop the unity of spirit and appreciation for each other's gifts, ministries, and activities that Paul discusses in his illustration about the body? There are no templates, no list of instructions, no shortcuts to achieve that.

Intimacy with God Fosters Unity with Others

FLORENCE

As you're spending time *being* with Jesus, seeking his heart and mind, when you run across another disciple who is also seeking Jesus, it could be that you're on the same path. Relationships and partnerships born out of unity in Christ are the very things he blesses. They are the things that bear fruit. As we join together in pursuing God's wisdom and direction, our unity attracts his blessing.

That doesn't mean it's easy to achieve unity. Sometimes a unified approach seems nearly impossible. The differences can be great between a Western church and an indigenous ministry; both partners may have widely different priorities and ideas of what God has called them to do. And achieving unity when partnering with a secular organization can often be very difficult and require careful discernment and discretion.

I had an experience like that when the US Agency for International Development (USAID) asked Life In Abundance to join them in working with a particular community to provide water and sanitation development. The government of that nation had recommended LIA to USAID, and we were honored to receive the praise of the national government. Wanting to remain in that government's good graces, we agreed to work with USAID, as long as they would be willing to run the project through the local church. USAID said that would be okay, but added, "We don't want to know about it."

They told us to refer to the church as a community-based organization and to reference only those aspects of the church's operations directly related to the development proposal we submitted. USAID does not fund spiritual work, but is geared to support development projects. They were clear that we could run the program as we wanted; they simply wanted to see results.

Sadly, there was no unity in that arrangement. The timing of reports seemed as important as the work itself to USAID. Their constant and unrelenting pressure—"Show us the results"—was beginning to harm our relationship and long-term partnership with the local church. So at the end of the three-year contract, we pulled the plug on our relationship with USAID, one of the largest funding partners in the world. The money just wasn't worth it. The disparity between our approach and theirs was harming our unity with the local church and disrupting the effectiveness of our ministry for the Kingdom of God.

You have to be careful. Just because an organization is willing to invest financial resources in your project doesn't necessarily mean you are receiving God's blessing. He has promised to command a blessing when his people are united, but it's difficult to achieve true unity when you are partnered with an unbeliever.

Unity Invites Diverse Insights

Unity does not mean all partners are always in agreement. There have been many times when Charlie and I have disagreed, and that is certainly true of us and our indigenous partner churches. Every relationship will have its differences of opinion. We need to hear different perspectives and have different voices speaking into our lives with messages that challenge our plans and the status quo. If we're hearing the same voices from the same perspective all the time, we won't grow.

I remember the early days of my medical ministry, when Festus and I worked among the Maasai villages in Kenya. The Maasai have an unusual cultural practice of consulting with others in their age group and then collaborating to reach a consensus. Festus was sharing Christ with them one day in a large meeting when they said, "We want to stop and discuss this."

They assembled into their age groups, and after some questions and dialogue they compiled the insights of the groups, and when they came back into the meeting with us, they said, "Okay, we have decided—we will all become Christians."

That was unity like I had never seen before!

The Global North and Global South need to listen to one another and learn from one another. Both have much to offer the other. Diverse voices give us a broader perspective and open our eyes to different ideas. That's why Jesus tells us to love one another, spend time with one another, hear one another, and live in unity with one another. A benefit of unity is that it builds trust—so your partners know that you will not swoop in like an eagle and take over—and gives us an opportunity to hear those different voices.

Jesus said, "Go therefore and make disciples of all nations. . . . And behold, I am with you always."[4] We may reply, "Okay, but I want to do it *my* way. I have this new, exciting strategy that I'm sure will work." The trouble is, if you do that, you'll be going it alone—and that's not the kind of unity God desires.

In those places and organizations where God's presence is sought and invited, Psalm 133 becomes a reality. God commands a blessing because he is present, dwelling in our unity and being glorified in it. When he commands a blessing, the work we accomplish in unity together will flourish.

Questions for Reflection and Journaling

1. When have you experienced the blessings that come from unity, partnership, and collaboration?

2. Which members of God's family do you find it difficult to work with in unity? Have you prayed and asked God to reveal the problem and show you how to resolve it?

3. Have you ever tried to work with another believer who had a completely different political or cultural affinity? How well did it work? Was unity difficult to achieve? How did you overcome your differences?

4. Do you have godly mentors to guide you in knowing which relationships are good to pursue?

5. How are you listening for God's leading and pursuing unity with others in your life right now?

17

FOLLOWING A STRATEGY

However beautiful the strategy,
you should occasionally look at the results.
AUTHOR UNKNOWN

In all your ways acknowledge him,
and he will make straight your paths.
PROVERBS 3:6

FLORENCE

I was asked to speak to a class called Perspectives on the World Christian Movement. Usually I teach the twelfth lesson, Christian Community Development, which is the beginning of the missions strategy section. Having taught this lesson many times, I fully intended to recycle the content I had used successfully the previous time. However, as I was preparing my lesson plan, I sensed a rebuke from God's Spirit saying, "Don't just copy and paste what you've presented before."

It was a busy time for me, and I was tired. In my weakness, I replied, "Lord, I'm teaching tomorrow, please be kind with me. Please don't tell me to come up with a whole new teaching." But I immediately knew that my plan was not his intention for the class. He had something better in mind.

After further prayer, I started thinking about what it takes for people to become effective in partnering with God to accomplish the Great Commission. I came to the realization that the key to being effective in God's plan for the world isn't better strategy. In fact, if I had to create a prioritized list of the key elements for reaching the world with the gospel and making disciples, strategy would be nowhere near the top.

Instead, God gave me some new insights to share and some important questions to ask the students. I still talked to the class about transformational development, but before I got to the strategic principles, I first needed to be certain my listeners had a strong spiritual foundation to adequately prepare them for service.

"Salvation is key—it's number one," I said. "Then the Great Commission tells us to go and make disciples, but how can you disciple someone if you haven't yet been discipled yourself? So first, you must *be* a disciple."

The beginning of that class was like a spiritual checkup: "Do you know Christ personally? Do you know him well enough to introduce him to others? Do you spend sufficient time with him so that you really know him intimately as a friend? Do you know his voice? You may think you have the best strategy, but if you are not flourishing in your relationship with Jesus, your strategy will fail."

As heads nodded in understanding throughout the room, the checkup continued: "Are you surrendered to God on an intimate level? Are you engaging in listening prayer to seek God's direction? Are you willing to endure personal sacrifice?" Those are necessary prerequisites for anyone who desires to do any productive work for God, and before launching any strategy that hopes to bear fruit.

Inspect the Foundations

The same principles apply to our partnerships. If you are working with people who have truly surrendered to Christ, they will not be pushing their own agenda; instead, they will be focused on the agenda of the King of kings. If both partners are surrendered to Christ, they can seek the Lord's guidance together—in unity. As both partners follow Christ, it's only natural they will find themselves on the same path together.

It is vitally important to know the spiritual foundation of any organization that wants to partner with you. Do they share the attributes and values that you prioritize? If the other party is pursuing their own agenda, the partnership will not thrive, because you are not both focused on following the path that God has prepared for you. But if you both have built on strong foundations that show an intimacy with God and dependence on him, then you can ask God for his direction and expect him to guide you.

The Birth of a Strategy

Years ago, Charlie and I both determined to make it a priority to ask God for his direction and his strategy for reaching the world and bringing real transformation to the whole person. As we continued to invest significant time in prayer and focused our attention on seeking him—surrendering everything to his control and laying ourselves before him in a sacrificial and prayerful way—he answered us time and again. As we followed his direction, he revealed a strategy that has borne lasting fruit.

This strategy is focused on dealing with the root causes of people's problems, through the work of the local church and indigenous leadership. We intentionally avoid doing or providing things that the community can do or provide for themselves, and thus we are careful to avoid creating dependency. Our programs can be sustained by the local community, and they produce lasting transformation over a three-year time span. From the very beginning, we have an agreed-upon exit plan clearly defined. And because this strategy was formed through our own intimacy with God, it allows us to follow his guidance when adjustments are needed.

But we need more than just a strategy in order to lead. Trusting relationships are a necessary precursor to strategy. Remember, it's *being* before *doing*. Our focus cannot be on creating and implementing the perfect strategy. But that's what so many organizations seem to hunger for. They want the blueprint without the foundation—a roadmap without having prepared for the journey.

A God-given strategy must be carried out by people who are earnestly and consistently seeking the Lord's direction. Two groups can employ the same exact strategy, but one ministry outcome might be life-giving while the other has little to no impact. The difference comes from maintaining an intimate relationship with God—a relationship that grows from quality time spent in his presence.

So many organizations already have a clear mission—or so they say; and thus they don't take the time to consult with God for further direction. I have heard people say, "We are not a prayer ministry; that isn't our calling. We are focused on providing clean water." Or "We are focused on stopping human trafficking, sponsoring children, building schools"—you can fill in the blank with any other good work. But it's the mission that Christ calls us into that he blesses—not our own mission that we invite him into. It's when God's people seek his direction and obey him in unity that Psalm 133 becomes a reality. That is where God commands a blessing, and where the work done in unity flourishes.

How do we develop relationships that will operate in unity? As Jesus says in the Sermon on the Mount, "Seek first the kingdom of God and his righteousness, and all these things will be added to you."[1] If you seek him, hear his response, and obey, the relationships, unity, and strategy will follow. A God-inspired strategy comes from actively seeking God.

The principles we've shared are the foundation of how we do the work of wholistic transformational development. The strategy is the systematic application of those principles under God's guidance.

What Our Strategy Looks Like

The work we do can be seen as five stages of walking with a partner community:

1. **Enter.** We start serving in a community with the Lord's guidance and set out to establish strong relationships with local pastors and community leaders. Then the local pastors facilitate vision-casting for their area.
2. **Empower.** We initiate sustainable programs in the community by equipping and training local church and community leaders in the methods of our wholistic development model.
3. **Establish.** We set up structures and systems for how people in the community will serve and implement projects to meet their needs in wholistic, sustainable ways.
4. **Expand.** We strengthen existing programs to equip other churches as the impact of the work reaches surrounding communities.
5. **Entrust.** After three years, we review the program to ensure that the local church and community leaders can take full ownership of the work and perpetuate its growth.

Here's how it works: At the very beginning, we pray. In God-honoring unity, we enter a new community to hear from him. We go in without any fanfare or presenting ourselves as experts; we simply go to pray for the people and for the churches. We ask God for his direction, for what he wants us to do—or not do. Our normal practice is to take prayer walks through the community. We see the needs and ask God to reveal his heart for these people. We pray about strongholds that need to be addressed spiritually, and we listen for God's direction and guidance.

If we believe God is leading us to work in this community, we'll invite the local pastors to a vision seminar, where we present the principles of transformational development.

The leaders learn what it takes to bring about sustainable, long-lasting change, and the central role of the church in that process. There is discussion about how to maintain healthy partnerships and how to instill ownership in the community for their own development. They begin to understand the steps involved in training, equipping, and empowering their people to be involved in serving the vulnerable and the poor.

We ask questions like these: "What do you believe God wants your community to be like? Are there areas that you think he wants to transform?" Over the course of three days, we help the leaders see that God has a plan for their community, and that it is the role of the local church to lead that ongoing process of transformation. We offer to come alongside the church for a limited time—three years—to train leaders who can train others, to provide limited resources to start the process and to be mentors, disciple-makers, and partners in the transformation of their community.

This three-year program duration provides a clear exit strategy that is known and agreed upon from the outset. It models the ministry of Jesus—he chose twelve men with no background in ministry or evangelism and transformed them through a discipleship process. In three years, he trained them to become trusted and empowered coworkers to whom he gave authority and power to continue his global work of redemption and transformation.

At the end of our initial time with local pastors and leaders, much like the vision seminar we described in Haiti, we pray and then ask the remaining pastors if they want to invite us into their community to help them bring about lasting change. If they say yes, we either arrange for an experienced trainer and leader to move into the community and spearhead the efforts, or we identify a trusted and respected local leader whom we disciple, train, and equip to be our local representative. We then raise up a local team to work with this leader. Together they train and disciple cohorts from churches throughout the region.

COMMUNITY OUTREACH STRUCTURE

In this management structure, the church is the center of activity, and the church has agreed to be the agent of change in the community.

The church is then trained in wholistic transformational development (WTD) and accepts ownership of the community's development.

The community leaders (people of peace) are invited to be trained and equipped by the church in WTD. A community committee is formed, consisting of nine members, half from the church, half from the community.

The community committee trains health promoters (one for every ten families).

The church trains spiritual health promoters (one for every ten families).

The community is mapped and divided into clusters (typically nine clusters of thirty to forty families each). Trained representatives are assigned to each cluster.

As WTD takes hold throughout the community, the church is seen as the leader in the transformation of the community.

Training and the Initial Seed Project

After the training has begun, we ask the local church leaders what they see as the primary felt need in the community. We then begin to pray and discuss ways to address that need. Out of that prayer comes an initial seed project. It's important for this initial project to be something that can be completed quickly and successfully so the community gains confidence in the process.

After that, we ask about the root causes of problems in the community. For instance, if the problem is how to deal with orphans and vulnerable children, we ask why the children are living on the streets, or why they are at risk in the community, and how the local church can respond to these needs. We help the church identify where the at-risk children are coming from. Then the church works to equip and empower single mothers, enabling them to take proper care of their children. They do it as a partnership with other women in the church so the single moms don't feel as if they are carrying the weight and responsibility all on their own. The church also establishes groups of caregivers, identifying and equipping families who are willing to take in one or more needy children. These care groups are formed with other mothers, grandparents, and friends, so there is strength that comes from a group being focused on the needs of the orphans and vulnerable children. Both the caregivers and the children are surrounded by people who want them to succeed and do well, and the church provides support and accountability.

Really, the easier way would be to build an orphanage funded by foreign child-sponsorship programs. You could bring all the children to one place and take care of them in an institutional setting, with a trained leader in charge. But that solution eliminates all the benefits of parenting. It ignores systems already in place in most of these communities and renders them useless. A program that allows children to stay with their family, or with another caring family in their community, is a far better long-term solution than placing them in an orphanage. As attention is focused on the root causes of why children end up on the streets or are not cared for by their family, those issues can be addressed and changes made—and then long-term transformation becomes a very real possibility.

The Importance of Finding and Fixing Root Causes

Here is an allegorical story that demonstrates the importance of finding the root cause of a problem and addressing the issue at that initial point instead of pouring resources into treating the outcomes of the problem:

There is a village somewhere with a river running through it. Along the riverbank, a group of people are fishing, as they often do.

Suddenly, they hear the cries of a person struggling out in the river, caught in the current and obviously in great distress. The fishermen drop their gear and form a human chain, grasping each other tightly as they wade into the river. They get close enough to the person to grab him and pull him to shore. Unfortunately, despite their heroic efforts, they are too late. The victim was underwater for too long and succumbs to drowning.

As time goes on, this same sad result happens time and again. Every time the group goes out to fish, it isn't long before they see another person out in the river, caught in the current and going under.

These drownings are obviously a very big problem that needs immediate attention. So the community organizes a rescue team to patrol the riverbank. They receive training to pull people from the river more efficiently and resuscitate them so they won't die. The program is an immediate success. Every day, the rescue team pulls people from the river, and many of them survive.

The people in the village realize that pulling victims from the river is vitally important, but too many people are still dying for lack of emergency medical care. So the community creates an ambulance service with an emergency vehicle posted at the river. As soon as people are rescued, the ambulance is ready to rush them to the hospital.

This new approach saves more lives, but some drowning victims die in the ambulance because the hospital is a fair distance away. So the compassionate people of the community raise the necessary funds to build an emergency medical clinic right on the riverbank. Now there is very little delay between pulling people from the water and getting them resuscitated and brought back to health.

The community feels great about all the lives they are saving, but they are so busy with their successful rescue operations that they never stop to wonder where all these people are coming from and why they keep ending up in the river.

Finally, a woman from the village takes a leisurely walk upstream along the river, and she eventually reaches another community just a short distance away. It's a larger town, with people living on both sides of the river, but there is no bridge across the stream. The only way to get from one side to the other is by carefully stepping from stone to stone along an established route. While the woman is watching, someone slips on the rocks, falls into the river, and is swept downstream by the strong current.

The woman realizes that these must be the people her community is working so hard to save. And it dawns on her that what they really need is a bridge that would allow the townspeople to safely cross the river.

Armed with this information, she hurries home and excitedly shares her discovery with everyone on the rescue committee. She tries to organize a construction team to partner with the neighboring community to build a bridge, but her friends are all too busy working to save the drowning victims. They tell her they don't have the time and resources to build a bridge because they are too busy saving lives! How could she pull them away from that important task to build a bridge in a community that isn't even theirs, for people they've never even met?

We need more people like that woman who walked upstream. We need people to ask the obvious question—"Why is this happening?"—and then find ways to solve the root problems.

God's way is better than our own devices. What a joy it was at the end of that three-year period to celebrate a cohort of children who had been brought into homes and families through the church. Children who were now being fed, clothed, and loved; who were going to school and being discipled—children with a hope and a future!

The Key Role of the Local Church

Over the course of the three years that we work in a community, we ask the question "Why is this happening?" many times. As a result, multiple projects are started and completed, all addressing the root causes of the community's felt needs. The solutions are all locally sourced. The local church provides leadership and management accountability. Trusted people from the church are selected and trained, and they in turn train other trainers. These key leaders help members of the community learn vital skills—about hygiene, health, food production and storage—and share with them the good news of the gospel of Jesus Christ.

Throughout the course of this partnership, we often remind the local church of the three-year duration of our presence, and we work diligently to empower and equip their leadership with everything they need to know to continue the work of transformation in the community after we leave.

People are drawn to the program because they see the changes in the lives of their neighbors; and they are drawn to the church because they see the dramatic transformation in the lives of Christians in their community. In fact, subsequent research has shown that the programs begun in these communities have not only continued, but have grown; and the local church has started even more programs.

And God receives the glory.

This Strategy Has No Shortcuts

At this point in our story, my concern is that many "results-oriented" leaders—particularly in the West—will read this, and as it starts to make sense, they'll pull out a notepad and start recording the actionable insights we've shared thus far, trying to craft a streamlined strategy they can adapt to their own ministry. If this describes you, you're in good company. I understand the desire to distill these principles into a handful of core practices and insert them into your current programs in an effort to be more successful. But here's what worries me: Others who have done the same thing have tended to copy only the *doing* elements, glossing over the *being* elements of the LIA strategy. They skim past the biblical foundational principles and focus on the practical, repeatable steps. They don't make the commitment to invest significant time seeking God and listening for his guidance. All they know is that their current strategy isn't producing the results they want, and they need something to fix it—so why not try *this*?

Charlie gave a talk to a group of leaders not long ago, and at the end of the presentation he shared one key lesson he had learned about how to have an impact in these indigenous communities. At the end of the session, the attendees were all coming up to him saying, "Yes! Thank you! That's what we're going to do. This meeting has been worthwhile because you gave us that strategy."

Charlie couldn't believe it. After all he had said throughout the session, the leaders had taken away very little of lasting value. They were only looking for a quick fix.

The temptation to turn these principles into a recipe or a template is huge. We understand that. But remember, it's not a template; it's a biblically based strategy. God rarely uses a template, but he is very strategic. He has plans, and he knows his plans. Our role is to join him in implementing those plans—*his* plans, not our own. And it starts with an investment in prayer and seeking his wisdom and guidance.

Too many ministries are focused on *getting something done* so they can show their donors a return on their investment. For Western leaders, the bias for action is a constant pull. They look for new ideas and better strategies to integrate into their work so they can get more done in a shorter amount of time. But copying a strategy and implementing it will not succeed unless it is built on a solid foundation of prayer and listening and collaboration with the local church—unless it is rooted in the constant desire to hear from God for the next step. Because at any moment, he may want you to do something different—maybe even radically different!

What If Three Years Isn't Enough Time?

In Haiti, we had made our normal three-year commitment to empower the churches to take responsibility for leading the ongoing development work in their community. But as the end of the third year approached, something seemed wrong. We asked God for insight, and we realized that, because of the many years of dependency created by the glut of foreign aid, the local church and community were not yet ready to take full ownership of their own development. We prayed earnestly about it, and we believed God was leading us to extend our initial exit timeline beyond the three years. This was highly unusual, so we earnestly persisted in prayer to be sure this was God's intention, and that we weren't simply making a mistake. We sensed God's clear direction and peace about the decision, so we stayed beyond the planned three years.

Six months into the extended time, we were able to see that lasting fruit was now being manifested; that the development projects undertaken were going to be sustainable; and that the local church would be able to continue discipling their people and leading the work of transformational development in the community. If we had dogmatically stuck with our strategy and said, "Sorry, but we have reached the three-year mark. Our job here is done. You're on your own. We're moving on," we would have missed seeing the ripening of the harvest. The fruit would not have matured, and lasting transformation would not have resulted.

That is a unique example, and there have also been times when we finished a bit earlier than expected. But the point is to make sure that ongoing prayer is a normal, integral part of your work so you can know with confidence when you need to alter your strategy along the way.

We're not talking about just starting your meetings with a short prayer, but for every person on the team to regularly and consistently seek God's wisdom and listen for his guidance—preferably in unity with your ministry partner.

We Need a Complete, Unified Body for the Work Ahead

As the global body of Christ, we need each other. We are not in competition with one another. We need to demonstrate our love for one another, because that's how the world will know we are followers of Christ.[2] Christian love is perhaps our most effective evangelistic tool.

Charlie and I come from two different cultures, two different backgrounds, but we share the bond of Christ. We have a deep admiration and respect for each other. Our relationship at times reminds me of what Paul said about his relationship with Titus: "When I came to Troas to preach the gospel of Christ, even though a door was opened for me in the Lord, my spirit was not at rest because I did not find my brother Titus there. So I took leave of them and went on to Macedonia."[3] Even though Paul found an open door for ministry in Troas, he did not stay there to work and share the gospel—because

Titus, his partner in ministry, wasn't there with him. That's how my partnership with Charlie has affected both of our ministries. That's why we've often gone into new areas together—two individuals, two ministries, but one Jesus, one mission, one partnership, and one goal.

God has a plan for the nations, but many of the partnerships and strategies in use today simply aren't working. In fact, they're actually taking us backward. So many ministry relationships are transactional in nature and do not exhibit mutual submission between true partners. Others are running their own show. Sadly, so many in the body of Christ—both in churches and ministry organizations—are competing instead of partnering.

When we see organizations that genuinely want to serve and glorify God, but are not seeing lasting fruit and genuinely don't know why their approach isn't working, we become motivated to help.

We have found something that works. It's having a lasting impact. It's attracting God's blessing. It's sustainable and reproducible. And that's why we want to share it with you.

Questions for Reflection and Journaling

1. Before honing your own missions strategy, ask yourself: Am I surrendered to God on an intimate level? Am I engaging in listening prayer to seek God's direction? Am I willing to sacrifice my own vision for what God wants?

2. What is God speaking to you about *being* with him before *doing* any strategy he might reveal to you?

3. Why do you think the LIA strategy has been successful? What do you see in it that's different from the strategies currently being used by other missions organizations? Why is the three-year commitment so significant?

18

PUTTING IT ALL TOGETHER

In essentials, unity;
in nonessentials, liberty;
in all things, charity.
MARCO ANTONIO DE DOMINIS

I therefore, a prisoner for the Lord, urge you to walk in a manner
worthy of the calling to which you have been called.
EPHESIANS 4:1

CHARLIE

I've made the drive thousands of times. Starting on the east side of Louisville—where Southeast Christian Church is located, where I had my dental practice, and where I live—I head west, passing many nicely renovated neighborhoods. Off to the left, I see the beautiful grounds of Churchill Downs, home of the Kentucky Derby, the most prestigious horse race in America.

Soon I cross Ninth Street—the economic and racial dividing line of the city. I'm entering one of the poorest zip codes in America, on my way to visit a friend, the Rev. Darrell Wilson, pastor of Greater New Beginnings Christian Church. He and I have been friends since I introduced him to the concept of wholistic transformational development.

On this day, as I get closer to the church, I notice all the homes that are either abandoned or dilapidated and in need of major repair. Later, in the church office, I mention it to Darrell, and together we get back in the car and drive the streets around the church. On our tour of the area, we count 129 houses that are abandoned or uninhabitable within a three-block radius of the church.

In Louisville, there is a wide gap between the wealthy and the poor—in fact, the average income of the top 20 percent of Louisville residents is more than fifteen times greater than the average income of the bottom 20 percent.[1]

In the past, some good organizations have run programs to help people in West Louisville get a home. Unfortunately, the houses were often abandoned again just a few years later, typically because the residents ran into financial problems and could no longer afford to stay.

Because Darrell and I both know the principles of wholistic transformational development, we can discuss and pray about this issue together with the same heart and mind. We know that loving the whole person in West Louisville includes helping these neighbors have a home—a safe and secure place to live. But this also means having the necessary income to provide for their families and escape the burden of debt. Darrell and I agree that any sustainable solution must come through the local church.

To our way of thinking, those 129 abandoned or dilapidated houses represent both a problem and an opportunity.

To address the issue, Greater New Beginnings Christian Church partnered with Southeast Christian Church and the Fuller Center for Housing. Over a two-year period, fourteen houses were rebuilt by volunteers from all three partner organizations—including sweat equity from the families that would move into them. Ten years later, the great news is that all but one of those families that worked to move into their homes still live there.

This project is an example of a sustainable, long-term, wholistic development solution to a problem that has beset impoverished communities in Louisville, and in most cities across America, for many, many years.

Prior to this renovation program, all fourteen beneficiary families could only rent a place to live. Studies have shown that owning a home helps a family build wealth. Their mortgage payments to purchase the homes (a twenty-year amortization with zero interest) were less than the rent payments they had been making previously.

Home ownership also helps these families socially because they now have a stable place to call home, where a sense of belonging to a community can be developed. The families were strengthened emotionally by not continually having to pack up and move from one rented place to another.

This project also met a felt need in the community by making it look like and become a better place to live. The esteem and social fabric of the community were built up as the residents realized that things were changing, and that other people now see their neighborhood as a desirable place to live.

Additionally, the local church benefited because they now had a group of families living close by who could be active in church life. People who lived near Greater New Beginnings Christian Church saw that it was actively involved in making the neighborhood a better place and helping people who lived there, so even the neighbors who didn't attend the church began to regard the church as relevant in their community life, and as a caring, loving, and compassionate group of people.

This was just the beginning of many projects the two churches did together to meet needs that were relevant to our community. This was possible because we held deeply the biblical principles of wholistic transformational development, and we were trusted friends who were free to disagree without dishonoring one another.

The Principles of Transformational Development in Action

Putting everything together begins by assessing our own lives as Christians, and our partnerships with others, as we seek to live out the core principles of transformational development. Humility is the key to all our relationships because we realize that none of us knows everything or has all the answers.

The apostle Paul tells us to "walk in a manner worthy of the calling to which [we] have been called."[2] We have been called by God, and thus we are to walk in accordance with his standards. As children of God, we belong to our heavenly Father and are part of his family. That tells us a lot about how we ought to live—not out of compulsion, but out of gratitude for all he has done for us.

God has "blessed us in Christ with every spiritual blessing."[3] He has redeemed us and forgiven us, given us wisdom and insight, and made known to us "the mystery of his will."[4] He has given us the inheritance he planned for us before the world began.[5]

He has given us resurrection power.[6] He has defeated death and made us alive again in Christ.[7] He has taken us who were far off, who were lost, who were cut off, and he has made us "a new creation" in himself.[8] He has given us the great mystery of the truth of the gospel, the truth of the church; and he's made it possible for us to capitalize on all of this by giving us his Holy Spirit, who strengthens our inner being so that Christ can be at home in our hearts. In the power of the Spirit, we can be filled with incomprehensible love; we can have internal satisfaction and joy, the fullness of God; and we can know his power. God has done all this for his own glory. He's done everything for us.

So how do we go about walking in a manner worthy of this calling?[9]

When the Christian life is characterized by the principles we've outlined, like spokes on a wheel, the hub that holds them all together is our devotion to intimacy with God. That intimacy is forged through prayer. We must remember to dwell in *seeking prayer*, listening to God and learning to hear his voice and obey him. And we mustn't go anywhere or do anything without praying about it first.

Then we must consider our actions, our works, from an eternal perspective—especially when engaging in any kind of missions activity. We must propagate the fruit that lasts in the lives of the people we serve, ensuring that they will be able to sustain the changes without outside assistance. We need the balance and inclusion of the Three C's—the Great Commission, Great Commandment, and Great Concern—if we are to love and serve the whole person as Christ does.

Matthew 25 gives a short list of the many problems we might need to address in loving the whole person. Identifying root causes and bringing biblical solutions is the responsibility of those who follow Christ. And according to this passage, we will be judged by how we respond to those needs.

Next is the wise use of immediate relief and long-term development—each in its appropriate place—with the goal of elevating and honoring those who are in desperate need and teaching them to develop sustainable skills that will help them and their families on into the future. The goal is to bring glory to God, not to ourselves.

That way of thinking leads to the principle of using short-term missions in ways that will strengthen local ministries and local churches—realizing that the short-term missions experience can be life-changing for the people who participate, but also wanting those efforts to be of lasting benefit to the people they serve. It's possible, and desirable, for both participants and recipients to be changed for the better through the STM experience.

One key principle we must always keep in mind is that working with the local churches and giving them program ownership is essential to long-term success in any area where we hope to have a positive, lasting impact. Remember, the church is the bride of Christ; and even though she isn't perfect, God has promised to bless the work done through her in unity.

Disciple-making follows, as we mutually disciple and learn from one another. As we grow in our understanding of God and his ways, we must be willing to mentor others. At the same time, we must realize that we still have a lot to learn, and as Westerners there is much we can learn from our brothers and sisters in the developing world.

Training and discipling local Christians in the areas where we've been called must become second nature to us, with the goal of working ourselves out of a job and turning over the work to the local community within three years. As we train the trainers, we know that the multiplication effect will have a much greater and longer-lasting impact than if we were to try to do all the work ourselves.

This is where the power of equal partnership comes in. As we collaborate in unity with other ministries and the local church, we demonstrate to a broken and hurting world the unity of fellowship that God himself experiences in the Trinity—and that he welcomes us into as his beloved children.

It is vitally important to maintain unity on the things that matter, and not to destroy our unity over things that really aren't important. As you begin partnering with other agencies, churches, and mission groups, you will have differences to work out. Financial accountability standards, leadership styles, past histories, denominational idiosyncrasies, and doctrinal differences will come into play. We need to know what is truly essential in our beliefs and where we can allow one another the freedom to interpret things differently. Some theological differences are extremely important in working together to serve the poor. For instance, we don't want to confuse the people we serve by collaborating with cults or nominal believers. But many differences in doctrine, interpretation, and practice are not important enough to compromise our ability to partner together—though they might affect our individual behavior.

We must be willing to sacrifice our own ambitions to serve God's purposes. Remember Paul's admonition in Romans 12:1-2:

> I appeal to you therefore, brothers, by the mercies of
> God, to present your bodies as a living sacrifice, holy and
> acceptable to God, which is your spiritual worship. Do
> not be conformed to this world, but be transformed by
> the renewal of your mind, that by testing you may discern
> what is the will of God, what is good and acceptable and
> perfect.

This is the *doing* part of our lives, our "spiritual service" (or "reasonable service," as some translations have it). In the same chapter, Paul encourages us to use our gifts to serve others and to love people genuinely. He instructs us not to be lazy, but to rejoice in hope, give to the needy, bless our persecutors, and show sympathy. All these are practical ways of living out our Christian faith.

But notice that before Paul says anything about what we're to do, he refers back to the eleven chapters of doctrine that precede chapter 12:

> I appeal to you therefore, brothers, by the mercies of God . . .
> ROMANS 12:1

These "mercies of God" include God's righteousness, the uselessness of law and works, the saving power of faith, peace with God, standing in grace, the promise of glory, the gift of love, the indwelling of the Holy Spirit, our adoption into God's family, reconciliation, union, slavery to Christ, deliverance from sin, freedom from judgment, sanctification, justification, glorification, security, and God's unfailing promises. On the basis of these great realities about God, which he has extended to us by grace, this is how we are to live: We are to present our bodies as a living sacrifice.

If we can agree with our ministry partners on these "majors," certainly we can allow each other freedom on the "minors."

The early church had many differences, yet Paul reminds the Galatians, "It is for freedom that Christ has set us free. Stand firm, then, and do not let yourselves be burdened again by a yoke of slavery."[10] That "yoke of slavery" can include our legalism over petty differences that hold us back from working together in partnership with otherwise like-minded Christians.

Philippians 2:1-3 says, "If there is any encouragement in Christ, any comfort from love, any participation in the Spirit, any affection and sympathy, complete my joy by being of the same mind, having the same love, being in full accord and of one mind. Do nothing from selfish ambition or conceit, but in humility count others more significant than yourselves."

Humility is the key to lasting partnerships. When we finally realize that none of us knows everything or has all the answers, we can extend grace and freedom to each other. Healthy partnerships give all parties an opportunity to grow, while clinging to the principles and beliefs each holds dear. When our focus is on glorifying Jesus and producing a lasting impact, we don't have to insist on doing things our way or the way we've always done them. Humility gives us flexibility in working together and a desire to honor others above ourselves.

As we've explored in these chapters on the principles of transformation, including the strategy God has given us, we hope you have come to understand that partnership is essential for the many parts of the body to work together as one. And we bring God glory when the different parts of the body work together in unity. The strategies we've outlined have proven to be effective in country after country, and we love to see them replicated in other settings.

In the next section, we'll share some examples of the fruit we've seen from exercising these principles and strategies, and we'll offer some insights to help you do the work of the Kingdom as you explore how to live and work in this exciting new wave of mission activity.

Questions for Reflection and Journaling

1. Which of the principles covered in this chapter are the most difficult for you to implement in your life or ministry—and why?

2. Which of the transformational principles outlined in this section have been most eye-opening to you? Which do you think would make a major difference in your ongoing ministry?

3. Following the principle of unity in essentials, liberty in nonessentials, and charity in all things, which people and organizations could and should you partner with?

PART 3

LASTING FRUIT

19

WHERE IS THE FRUIT?

You can count the seeds in an apple,
but you can't count the apples in a seed.
AUTHOR UNKNOWN

All that I have heard from my Father I have made known to you.
You did not choose me, but I chose you and appointed you that you
should go and bear fruit and that your fruit should abide.
JOHN 15:15-16

FLORENCE

My husband, Festus, and I recently moved out of Nairobi and now live in a more rural area of Kenya. Our property includes various fruit trees. It is wonderful to watch the fruit grow and ripen, and then we enjoy it as food. The joy of having a fruit tree is seeing the process of growth and delighting in the harvest. It would be silly for us—or anyone else—to keep a fruit tree that never produced any fruit.

Jesus lived in an agrarian culture, and he talked quite often about fruit. He used it as a metaphor for results, impact, and outcomes—things that are produced by or grow from our lives and our work. Most people no longer live close to the land, so a bit of explanation may be in order before we talk about the fruit that results from applying agricultural principles in our work for God.

Fruit Should Be Expected

Farmers plant apple trees in full expectation of reaping a repeated harvest of apples, but it is not simply a "plant it and forget it" kind of activity. First, the small sapling is planted in a prepared hole where it will get adequate sun and won't be crowded by other trees or structures as it grows. It is watered, fertilized, and tended throughout the year. During this time there is growth but no fruit, because the tree is still immature. After another year or two of cultivation, the first apples finally appear. The wise farmer removes those small apples so that the tree's energy can be reserved to strengthen and prepare it for larger yields in future growing seasons. This process continues until the apple tree has been fully established in the ground for at least three years. By then the tree is usually mature enough to start bearing healthy, delicious fruit, year after year after year.

Even then, the farmer still works with the tree—fertilizing to ensure it has the nutrients needed to thrive, pruning weak branches, applying treatments to ward off pests that would harm the fruit, and ensuring an adequate supply of water. Every successive year, the tree grows larger and stronger, and the harvest of apples arrives every autumn, with more apples produced than the year before.

That's what Jesus is talking about in John 15:16, when he tells his disciples that he has chosen them to go and bear fruit—not just one harvest, but multiple harvests. Fruit that will abide. Long-lasting fruit. Repeated, sustainable harvests of fruit.

Earlier in John 15, Jesus says to his followers, "By this my Father is glorified, that you bear much fruit and so prove to be my disciples."[1] Just as an abundant harvest of fruit is proof that a grape branch "abides" in the vine, spiritual fruit—fruit that remains—is evidence that we are abiding in Christ Jesus; that is, we prove to be his disciples if we bear much fruit.

In order to recognize fruit, we must know what it looks like.

On the day after his triumphal entry into Jerusalem, Jesus was walking with his disciples from Bethany back to Jerusalem. Along the way, he noticed a fig tree with leaves and hoped to find some figs to pick, because he was hungry. Unfortunately, there was no fruit on the tree. In what seems to be an out-of-character reaction, Jesus curses the tree, causing it to wither completely.[2]

After seeing the fruitless tree, Jesus found the Temple crowded with people making money instead of praying and worshiping God, and he was confronted by religious leaders who challenged his authority and denied his divinity.

In each of these cases, there was no fruit found in places that appeared to be fruitful. The chief priests, scribes, and elders were seen as religious leaders, and yet they did not bear the fruit of righteousness. Neither could they recognize the Son of God in their midst. The crowds had gathered in the Temple, supposedly to prepare to celebrate their salvation and deliverance from Egypt in the first Passover; but instead this watershed event in their history had deteriorated into a fruitless tradition and a money-making opportunity for merchants in the Temple. The tree *looked* mature, but it had no figs.

Jesus clearly demonstrated that he expects fruit—cursing the fig tree, throwing the merchants out of the Temple, overturning the tables of the money changers, and confounding and condemning the religious leaders.[3] It's not enough to merely *appear* as if we are producing fruit. In our lives, and in the work we do for him, Jesus wants us to actually bear good, desirable, and lasting fruit.[4]

Just as Jesus looked at the fig tree and wanted to see sweet, ripe figs—good fruit—we want to see fruit in the communities where we have invested three years of work. And we have not been disappointed.

How to Recognize Good Fruit

Remember Almaz, the woman with leprosy I met during language school in Ethiopia? One of the many indicators of transformation in her life was *joy*. Christ dramatically changed her life and her family's lifestyle, and it was obvious to anyone who saw her face. Despite the disfiguring symptoms of leprosy, this widowed single mother had an inner glow because the love of Jesus had taken up residence within her. As a result, everything else in her life had changed as well.

As we prepare to leave a community and entrust the ongoing development process to the able hands of the local church, we know what fruit to look for as evidence of sustainable transformation.

We expect to see people who were previously hopeless now full of hope; those who were despondent with grief now possessing a spirit of hope; and those who were sad and downtrodden now having faces that reflect the presence of God's Spirit. We expect to see those who were in bondage now set free; shame replaced with dignity; broken relationships restored; children living with families and not on the street; those who were poor now self-sufficient; and children in school, preparing for the future instead of begging for food to eat today. Those who were sick, we expect to have renewed health, and those who were stigmatized by AIDS or leprosy now accepted as neighbors. We expect to see the local church growing and taking ownership of community issues. And we expect to see unity among the leaders of the churches. We expect to see the community coming together, interacting and participating in events and projects together. And we expect everything to look better—the trash gone, homes in better repair, the environment respected, and resources not wasted.

We expect to see these signs of transformation because that is what we have seen so many times before, in so many locations and circumstances. The fruit is proof that the principles and practices of wholistic ministry and developmental transformation *work*.

Unfortunately, many Christian ministries don't have much fruit to show for all of their labors. If that's true of you and your ministry, if your work isn't producing a lasting impact—fruit that endures—we recommend that you revisit the principles we shared in part 2. We have found that they lead to lasting fruit. The challenges of ministry are often complex, multifaceted, and requiring discernment. If you rush in with a solution already in mind, it's unlikely you will see lasting fruit.

Causes of Fruitlessness

There are many symptoms one might observe in ministries that are not producing lasting fruit. As you examine your own core practices and beliefs, honestly consider whether prayer is truly foundational to your ministry. Does it permeate every aspect of your life and influence your decisions? As you look at the activities of your work, whose glory are you seeking?

It's hard not to notice who gets the praise or who is lifted up as the hero in any kind of missions activity. Ministries that love being in the spotlight and taking credit for their projects tend to be more interested in growing their organizations and building their brand than in building the Kingdom of God. They may seem to be flourishing because they attract the attention of donors, but they do not attract the blessing of God. Despite the heart-gripping stories they tell of the work they accomplish, the fruit they produce is typically fleeting.

You can see the red flags in the relationships these ministries have with churches or other organizations. Their idea of partnership is more of a transaction than a relationship. It isn't mutually beneficial; instead, the in-country partner simply receives whatever the donor ships to them, uses or distributes it, and sends back photos and videos of the grateful local recipients.

Organizations focused on transactional relationships naturally seek projects that please people, rather than pursuing what pleases God. A ministry leader could say, "Our new strategy brought in $100,000 in donations, so God is obviously blessing this effort." But the true measure of blessing is not in fundraising. Are people coming to know Christ? Are they being discipled? Are lives being transformed? Are you demonstrating your love and concern for the whole person? Is the local church the primary vehicle of transformation? Is God getting the glory? These are questions that will help you determine whether your ministry is bearing fruit—not just immediate fruit, but sustainable, ongoing fruit.

Another symptom of a ministry that is not bearing lasting fruit is the tendency to chase trends and employ the latest hot strategies—strategies that fall by the wayside when the next big thing comes along. These strategies fade away because they don't produce lasting fruit; they weren't initiated by God, and therefore they don't attract his blessing. When you see missionaries returning home after a short time on the field, ask yourself, "Why is this happening? Are they burned out? Is the work they spent years preparing for—raising support, learning a language, and transitioning to a new culture—no longer relevant? Why did it not bear fruit?"

The key is observing and then asking, "What is God blessing, and what is he not blessing?" Hold fast to the first and reject the second.

Do What Results in Fruit

God is making two paths abundantly clear—either you can remain entrenched doing something that is not bearing fruit, or you can seek God wholeheartedly and listen intently to discover what he is blessing. You can unite with like-minded people to see lasting fruit come from your labors for God. He blesses what he births, and that birthing of new things results from prayer. What he gives birth to, he watches over to ensure it succeeds.

The promise Jesus makes at the end of the Great Commission is clear: "I will be with you." So as we go and make disciples, we have the assurance of his constant presence to lead, guide, and help us in every situation we face. Take advantage of the many benefits of that relationship—God's presence—that assures us of being in his will and doing what he desires.

That doesn't mean there won't be challenges or temporary set-backs, or that we don't need to work hard. It's simply that when we follow the principles outlined in God's Word, we can expect him to move in ways that bring fruit to our lives and glory to himself.

Be Ready to Pivot When God Directs

We need to be able to recognize the sense of God's favor on the work he is blessing, and also be able to sense when he is not blessing something we're doing. When God's presence and blessing have departed from a project or an organization, it's time to find out why. As we seek God's guidance, we must resist the pull of inertia—the urge to continue doing what God says to change—and not try to resuscitate or sustain old, fruitless works in our own power. Instead, let's move rapidly into what God wants to bless next.

What worked yesterday may not be what works today, and God's strategies will almost certainly change in the future. But the principles of God's Kingdom do not change. Examine the effect your work is having. If you're not seeing lasting fruit, go back and evaluate whether you and your ministry are in alignment with biblical principles.

In the next few chapters, you will read stories of lasting fruit that came from our partnerships, as well as an impact assessment report compiled by an objective outside research agency. We're sharing these reports not to show how amazing Life In Abundance is, or our strategy; or how well Southeast Christian Church selects and invests in indigenous partners. We're simply illustrating how this model of sustainable, God-directed, transformational development produces long-lasting fruit. And it can be true for *your* ministry too!

To God be all the glory.

Questions for Reflection and Journaling

1. What factors do you think are most important to assess the lasting fruit in your life and ministry? What evidence do you see of God's abundant fruit in your life right now?

2. Which of your current endeavors do you sense God is *not* using or blessing for his Kingdom?

3. What new things is God whispering to you that he would like to bless in your life and ministry? What next steps can you take to follow him in these new projects?

20

STORIES OF FRUIT

The fruit of the Spirit wasn't intended to be a list of goals for us to produce—it is the Holy Spirit through us who produces fruit.
DAN KIMBALL

The fruit of the righteous is a tree of life, and whoever captures souls is wise.
PROVERBS 11:30

FLORENCE

I sometimes wonder: *If I hadn't slogged through the sticky mud into that little church in Ethiopia—many years and fourteen countries ago—how would things be different today?* I still remember that Christmas Eve, my reluctance, and God's clear voice directing me to humbly ask for help from the local church. I have to wonder: If my eyes had never been opened to receive the transformational development paradigm, would I ever have started an international organization focused on long-term development by working through local churches? But my eyes *were* opened, and now we have so many stories to tell!

Creating a sustainable ecosystem in a community to allow for ongoing sustainable transformation is, in and of itself, fruit; but it also results in *ongoing harvests* of fruit. Here, and in the next few

203

chapters, are some examples of sustainable fruit from different parts of the world.

Multiplying Fruit in Haiti

We started by telling you about Haiti and how we first heard from God in that place of such desperate need. After three and a half years of working with the local churches, we finally saw lasting fruit and knew they were ready to take full ownership of their own development. Haiti is no stranger to tropical storms, experiencing the damaging impact of an average of fourteen to twenty-one named storms (winds of 39 mph or more) between June 1 and November 30 each year, of which six to ten could become hurricanes (winds of 74 mph or more).[1] Not long after the LIA team left that community in 2014, another hurricane hit that island nation. We contacted the leaders in the local church to see what their plan was. They told us they were ready and could handle it on their own . . . and they did.

They provided clean water for the first couple of days until the main water supply was repaired. Then they told the community it was time to work to rebuild what had been destroyed. They took the aftermath of the storm as an opportunity to improve their homes and businesses. Now they have grown to the point where they are taking the principles they have learned—and which have borne great fruit in their community—to other nearby villages to train others just as they were trained. As a result, they are seeing transformational development multiplied throughout their region.

Table Banking Fruit

Remember the pastor who was reaching for his wallet to help a single mother in a very poor part of Kisumu, Kenya? Fortunately, his local missions partner stopped him to avoid derailing the development process that was underway.

This widow had become a Christian through the outreach of the local church and had received training on how to generate income to provide for her family. She was very sick with HIV/AIDS and had three young children, so she knew she had to do something to change their desperate circumstances.

After receiving a small loan from the table bank she had joined at the church, she used it to start a micro-business, making and selling french fries on the street just outside the door of her tiny home. As the business became more successful, she added fish to the menu—so now passersby could get a quick meal of fish and chips!

By the end of LIA's three-year participation in that community, her business was thriving. Many customers were buying from her stand, and she was able to provide for her children and pay the school fees so they could get an education. Plus, she was able to pay back the loan. The last time I saw her before we left, she wore a broad smile of joy, accomplishment, and healing. She had begun a new AIDS treatment and was doing well physically.

Five years later, some members of our team went to visit her and were told she was no longer there. It was disappointing. What could have happened to her? As we kept asking more people who had known her, we discovered that her original french fry and fish stand had moved to a permanent kiosk, and she had started a second business—a shop that sold and repaired bicycles. Because bikes are used extensively in that town for personal transportation, she had a lot of customers. When we found her, she was thrilled! She exuded joy and self-confidence, and she looked like a totally different person than the woman the American pastor had met in that tiny shack years before.

One of the fruitful outcomes we see in every case where a person has been transformed: Not only has their situation changed, but now they see themselves as a different person. This woman no longer saw herself as a victim, ostracized by the community. She no longer saw herself as hopeless, unable to care for her children, and dependent on handouts to survive. She now realized that she was a child of God—capable of being a good mother and giving her children a healthy life. It was a transformation that began in her heart, spread to her mind, and was now written all over her face. Her transformation truly resulted in a complete rebirth. The old had passed away, and everything had become new!

A Harvest in a Difficult Place

The closed country where God led us to meet the church leader Farah Ali at the World Bank building has seen tremendous progress. The underground churches there are growing and seeing many lives changed, and communities are being transformed as a result of their partnership with LIA. The churches formed a charitable organization to teach the principles and practices of wholistic transformational development to the secular community—most of whom would be very hostile to an open proclamation of the gospel—and amazing change has resulted. In fact, the national government has repeatedly renewed the organization's registration, allowing them to continue their work because of the obvious impact it has and the far-reaching, lasting change that has resulted.

In the past year alone, the local church leadership has worked to empower two new underground churches to help poor and vulnerable people find lasting change, and they have formed three new cell group churches—all in secret! Their next goal is to empower ten more churches by training their leaders in wholistic transformational development.

Unexpected Fruit

CHARLIE

The organization we mentioned that was focused on relief efforts, such as packing and delivering container loads of emergency food, has changed its operating model since working with Life In Abundance. They have seen how the relief supplies they provide can be an important part of bringing a community out of a disaster, and they have realized it is equally important to stop relief when it is no longer necessary so that the work of transformational development can begin. They now look to work more with organizations, like LIA, that have a focus on sustainable transformation in a community so the people they serve will no longer need emergency relief.

This organization had also previously encouraged long-term child sponsorship programs, until they realized that the positive effects were temporary and the relief created dependency. Now they have put a three-year cap on sponsorship programs in order to give recipient families time to learn and apply biblical principles to help them become self-sufficient and no longer in need of outside financial support. In fact, when they told the local churches in one community that they were phasing out of sending money to pay children's school fees, the churches created a way to fund those school fees from within the local community and keep their kids in school—another great example of a local church taking ownership of their community's development. As that organization has been transformed and has significantly changed their missions approach to providing relief, they now realize the importance of transitioning to transformational development.

Fruit in Impoverished Cities

I also mentioned how Southeast Christian Church and the predominantly Black churches in West Louisville used to have a serious problem relating to one another. SECC was viewed as a church full of wealthy, white suburbanites, whose presence wasn't welcomed by the Black churches, and members of SECC tended to view the Black churches in West Louisville as having little effect in a community full of serious problems.

After much prayer, and after Life In Abundance sent a representative to live in Louisville and work with the various churches to learn and implement the principles we outlined in part 2, long-standing walls of separation were broken down and fellowship and joint ministry resulted. Today, a sweet friendship has grown between the pastors at Southeast Christian Church and the West Louisville pastors. They meet for monthly prayer together, they demonstrate mutual respect, and their churches have been empowered to partner in healthy ways. This is a wonderful testament to how the principles of transformational development work across very different cultures—even in the US! Short-term teams have now come alongside this effort to further strengthen the local churches in Louisville. That kind of unity and partnership never would have happened—despite years of effort—without applying the principles of sustainable transformational development.

A Harvest of Eternal Fruit

Yurian is a Cuban pastor who emigrated to the United States in 2001. Upon arrival he immediately began going out in his community to talk to people about Jesus. He built a house group that soon grew into a church. He has since planted ten churches made up of people from Mexico, Honduras, Guatemala, Cuba, and other Latin countries—including the largest Hispanic church in Louisville! That's how I first heard of him. I introduced Yurian to the principles of transformational development, and after being trained, he began using the material in his work in the community,

"As I go door-to-door," he later told me, "I get to know people and build relationships. I learned that the Bible is not the only tool we can use to open doors—the door to a person's heart or the door to a family. I started using the other transformational development tools—focusing not only on the spiritual side, but also on the relational, physical, and emotional aspects of a person's life."

Yurian says he now realizes that, in addition to their spiritual needs, the people he is reaching need to know what to do when their family is hungry, when they can't pay their bills, or when they don't have anybody who can translate for them at a doctor appointment. Those are the areas that the church sometimes neglects.

He has seen the principles of wholistic ministry open doors with individuals and with families. He has seen our approach connect with people who have never heard the gospel. After building relationships and trust over time, these people come to see that the church really cares about them, and about every problem they face. They want that same love to be in them, so they often become believers in Jesus. That's when the real transformation can begin!

The training (which they call Neighborhood Transformation) gives people a wholistic and complete model of transformation. "Sometimes," Yurian says, "people just need a friend."

When newcomers visit Pastor Yurian's church, he asks them, "How did you hear about us? Often they reply, "Everyone says that if you call here, you'll get help."

All the churches he has planted have been trained in living and ministering by these principles, and they all know how to pass them along to others—multiplying the impact throughout the Hispanic population of Louisville. In each location, the leaders understand that the church is like a hospital, expecting patients with needs to come through the door. Thus the church is prepared to help spiritually, physically, relationally, and emotionally—reaching, loving, and transforming the whole person.

Reaping Where We Did Not Sow

FLORENCE

From the humble beginnings of Life In Abundance while Festus and I were working in Ethiopia, the ministry spread to the neighboring African countries. Today, we have offices and success stories in fourteen nations. Beyond that, we hear reports of communities that have been transformed by putting the principles of transformation into practice—throughout Africa, Asia, and other parts of the world. We didn't go into those other nations to see if God had work for us to do there; he simply spoke to his people as they put *being* before *doing*, and they obeyed. The growth we've seen is its own fruit. God planted strategic seeds, and we are reaping the harvest.

And the Fruit Continues ...

Next, we'll look deeper into some stories of lasting fruit in three unique settings—rural Kenya, urban Ethiopia, and Africa's largest slum—where the principles and practices of transformational development have been tested, proven, and analyzed.

As you read these next stories, rejoice with us that God is at work producing lasting fruit—changing lives and transforming communities for his honor and glory!

Questions for Reflection and Journaling

1. How do you see the principles of transformational development reflected in the stories in this chapter?

2. What ideas have come to mind of ways you can see more lasting fruit in your ministry?

3. When you seek God about the fruit you see resulting from your work for him, what insights or direction does he give you?

21

FRUIT IN A RURAL COMMUNITY

The opposite of poverty is not wealth;
the opposite of poverty is enough.
WESS STAFFORD

He turns a desert into pools of water,
a parched land into springs of water.
PSALM 107:35

FLORENCE

Life is extremely difficult in the rural town of Makueni, in south-central Kenya. The ground is hard and dry in this semiarid region—so parched that it's marked by deep cracks and the broad riverbed is empty, covered with dry sand. This is not the best place to grow crops, but farmers try to grow maize, beans, and a few other vegetables on their small plots. The region has a short rainy season, so the crops often grow poorly, and the harvest is scarce. To make matters worse, it's not unusual for Makueni to miss a rainy season or two altogether.

People in Makueni have long struggled to grow enough food for their families. Grain is the primary staple, but when there's a good harvest, they've had no way to store enough grain to last through the lean months. Grain stored for later use would often be destroyed by weevil infestations.

But severe poverty and malnutrition are not the only problems. According to one local pastor, the Rev. Shadrack Kyumwa, the spiritual issues in Makueni have compounded the economic problems.

At the request of the local churches, Life In Abundance went to Makueni to assess the needs. After prayer-walking throughout the town and taking time to listen for God's wisdom and direction, we met with the local church leaders. At the close of that initial vision meeting, eleven area churches made a three-year commitment to partner with us. Food and water insecurity were the key initial needs identified by the leadership. Together, they agreed that providing large metal silos for safe and pest-free grain storage at each church would keep the farmers from having to sell their grain when prices were low—which was their usual practice in order to recoup some value from the grain before it could be spoiled and rendered worthless by weevils—only to have to buy grain in the market to feed their families when supplies were low and prices were high. By using silos, they could preserve their grain for their own needs, and also sell some of it for income when prices were high.

LIA provided the initial funding for silos to be located at the local churches. Pastor Titus Kweleva told us that the ability to store their grain without fear of loss made a tremendous difference for the people he serves.

"They work hard growing their crop and are happy knowing it will provide for their families even if there is a period of no rain."

LIA also helped the community start a table bank so that members could start new income-generating businesses. A table bank first introduces members to the benefits of saving money and enables them to take out small loans to help make their farms and shops more efficient and productive.

Joshua Muthusi is one resident member who took out a loan from the table bank to buy a gas-powered pump, allowing him to draw water from under the dried-up riverbed to irrigate his farm. The results were dramatic.

Joshua explains, "The river had been dry for six months, but I kept digging until I found water again." From that shallow well in the riverbed, Joshua now pumps water to irrigate a variety of crops. Today, his farm is thriving, producing more than enough for his family and plenty to sell at the market. He quickly paid back the loan for the pump and then took out another loan—this time to buy a motorcycle to help him transport his vegetables to the local market.

When Joshua's neighbors and relatives saw the huge change in his family's well-being, they started asking him what he was doing to make money and take care of his family. He told them that his church had helped him learn new business ideas and farming techniques. He also told them how a loan from the table bank had enabled him to irrigate his farm, which in turn made it possible for him to feed his family, pay for school fees, and have enough in savings to get safely through bad times. Joshua's simple testimony and the visible improvement in his farm attracted many people to the church to learn about Jesus and experience his abundant life.

Pastor Titus says that Joshua is now a leader in the church youth group and a wonderful example of what God is doing in the community. Joshua gives all the glory to God.

"Some people in my area now call me pastor," he says. "When I hear this, I thank God very much."

Pastor Shadrack also took out a loan from the table bank at his church for his wife to open a small shop, and that income is now enabling him to attend college to finish his studies.

Another church member, Vilia Mutie, asked her pastor and church leaders to pray with her to dedicate the ground she had purchased with a small loan. She is building a shop in the town center to help support her children and her disabled husband.

The chairman of the table bank, Reuben Mutunga, was selected by the community because of his smart business sense. He said this project turned his life around.

"I found Christ as my Savior because of what I saw happening here."

The transformation in Makueni has continued and has expanded throughout the region. Several years after LIA finished its three-year commitment there, the local churches united to build a large warehouse to store even more grain and help many more families. And the results continue to multiply in the lives of the people in the community. The table bank is still going strong—the residents are taking out loans and also saving money. Their table bank is named Beulah, which means, "This land will not be desolate again."

We thank God that the community of Makueni now has hope and a road to lead them out of desolation and into the abundant life.

Questions for Reflection and Journaling

1. How does this story resonate with you and give you ideas for your own life and ministry?

2. The church in Makueni undertook many projects that were not focused on spiritual transformation, but as a result of the testimony of people whose physical lives were changed, people were drawn to the church. How could similar things happen in your church?

3. What is God speaking to you through this story about the next steps you should take?

22

FRUIT IN A CAPITAL CITY

*Overcoming poverty is not a gesture of charity. It is an act
of justice. It is the protection of a fundamental human
right, the right to dignity and a decent life.*
NELSON MANDELA

*The LORD your God is God of gods and Lord of lords, the great,
the mighty, and the awesome God, who is not partial and takes
no bribe. He executes justice for the fatherless and the widow,
and loves the sojourner, giving him food and clothing.*
DEUTERONOMY 10:17-18

FLORENCE

Addis Mercato, the largest open-air market in Africa, is a hectic, smelly place. The loud, chaotic, crowded marketplace, sprawling across several square miles, is teeming with people and animals, all jostling to get past one another. There you'll find more than seven thousand shops and stalls and small businesses. The Mercato (which means *market*) is also a major transportation hub for trains and buses. Tens of thousands of extremely impoverished people live in and around the market area. They've come hoping to somehow obtain enough money to have a future—or at least to live another day.

Young teenagers escaping the rural provinces, where their families are very poor, often arrive in Addis Ababa without any contacts for work or a place to live—only the hope of finding a better life. Finding nothing of the sort, they make their way to the market, where they often become street thieves just to survive. This area is notorious for crime, especially robbery and prostitution.

As you can imagine, this vulnerable population living together in such close quarters has many health problems. Contagious diseases such as AIDS spread like wildfire. Many people lack even the basics of life in their tiny, scavenged shelters.

The marketplace is also an area of intense spiritual warfare.

Pastor Getahun Tadesse of the Emmanuel United Church in the Mercato area says the streets and alleys around his church are dangerous, full of young people who prey on both resident shoppers and the tourists who venture there. The churches have struggled against a lot of opposition, says Pastor Tadesse. It has been difficult for Christians to even exist in that troubled area, let alone have a noticeable impact.

The churches in the Mercato area heard about the success that Life In Abundance was seeing in other parts of the capital city, and they asked us to partner with them in finding ways to reach their community. Overwhelmed by the need, some churches were afraid to even reach out to the street gangs and prostitutes in the area.

LIA agreed to partner with Emmanuel and other churches in the Mercato for three years. LIA project coordinator Dereje Geane in Addis Ababa shared that one of the first needs the churches identified was to help single mothers make a living to support their kids and pay for school fees, shelter, and food. A sewing project was started with a local woman named Tanange leading it. The ladies learned to sew beautiful bed coverings and other items that could be sold in the Mercato. The sewing project not only helped the seamstresses economically, but it also gave them a support system that helped the church reach out to other vulnerable women in the community and help them spiritually as well. The sewing project also enabled Tanange to support herself and her two little boys after her husband died.

During the three-year LIA involvement and in the years since, many lives have found transformation in this place of hopelessness, despair, and danger.

For instance, Desta was only twelve when she came to the capital city in search of a job and a better life. Her mother had died and her father married another woman, who had her own children to support. Desta was told they could no longer afford her schooling, so she left home to fend for herself. For ten years, Desta lived on the streets, earning money any way she could, eventually turning to prostitution. Her health was faring poorly.

Then she decided to marry a man named Yohanna, who also lived on the streets. Yohanna was often abused in the Mercato because he was disabled and couldn't walk. He and Desta faced daily rejection and ridicule, even from fellow street people, as Desta lovingly carried him from place to place and cared for him. In faithfulness to her husband, Desta stopped selling her sexual services, and together they had two children.

Desta connected with LIA through a health clinic in the Mercato, and she invited the team to come meet her husband in the tiny place where they lived. The care and compassion they received ministered to her deepest needs. Now Desta attends a weekly Christian discipleship class, and her two daughters are involved in an economic empowerment project—as well as competing for the award of being the best performing student in their school.

Through LIA and the local churches, Desta has received business training, and she drew up a business plan to receive a microloan as start-up money to begin a small shoe business.

Soon she was able to buy her husband a wheelchair so he could get around on his own. He now goes to the market with Desta to buy, sell, and repair shoes. As a family, they have been empowered and transformed. They recently had a church wedding to bless their marriage.

There is so much fruit coming from this desperate place!

Another young person, Dawit, came to the Mercato area from one of the outlying provinces of Ethiopia at the age of thirteen. He had been kicked out of school, and his mother was very sick—too weak to care for both herself and her son. In the Mercato, Dawit ended up as a street boy, stealing whatever he could to survive. But then, through the ministry of the local churches, his life was turned around. He met Christ, went back to school, and even graduated from college to become a science teacher! He's now working as a teacher and assisting people as a volunteer in the Mercato.

The churches in the Mercato that were so small and fearful of the darkness and crime around them are now packed out each week with former street boys and prostitutes whose lives have been transformed. They have gained respect in that difficult neighborhood and are making a lasting difference in people's lives.

Questions for Reflection and Journaling

1. How does this story touch your heart and resonate with you?

2. Which of the people described here do you think most represent the concept of lasting fruit?

3. How do you think God might use your current ministry to produce the same kind of fruit?

23

FRUIT IN AFRICA'S LARGEST SLUM

Where you live should not determine whether you live, or whether you die.

BONO

Who is like the LORD our God, who is seated on high, who looks far down on the heavens and the earth? He raises the poor from the dust and lifts the needy from the ash heap.

PSALM 113:5-7

FLORENCE

It's a cold morning in the Kibera slum. The quiet room in the back of the health clinic begins to come alive as the transformational development agents arrive. They greet each other warmly. One woman holds her baby in a brightly colored cloth slung across her chest. You can feel the energy swell as they enter.

Kibera is one of the most desperately poor slums in the world. It is located in Nairobi, Kenya, just a few miles from the city's business and financial center. The constant influx and movement of residents makes it impossible to accurately count the population, but official estimates range from half a million to well over one million people, making it the largest urban slum on the continent of Africa.[1]

Most of Kibera's residents left their rural homes in hopes of finding an easier life and higher income in the capital city. Precious few achieve that dream; the majority eventually succumb to living out their days in the slum, scraping out a hand-to-mouth existence.

Tiny, cramped shanties provide basic shelter alongside open sewers. The stench is overpowering. Disease is rife in Kibera, and the medical clinics that operate there are overwhelmed by the number of people they have to treat. Malaria and TB are widespread. Assault and rape are common. A great majority of those living in the slum lack access to basic services, including electricity, running water, and indoor toilets.

Those who try to survive in Kibera are caught in a cycle of poverty that spans generations. Once you find yourself living there, escape seems almost impossible. But it's not just the issue of economics that holds people in bondage.

Pastor Michael, a local church leader, says the people of Kibera are also in desperate spiritual need—witchcraft, superstition, and crime have made it very difficult to minister there.

When Life In Abundance went to Kibera to prayerfully assess the needs, local church leaders from different denominations invited us to partner with them to see God bring transformation to this desperate place. Rarely had these churches worked together before.

Because most people who live in Kibera exist in extreme poverty, earning less than two dollars per day, the initial felt need identified by the church leaders was a money-making enterprise to help their members afford food, shelter, and school fees. Together, a shoemaking project was launched.

Life In Abundance taught the business and financial principles of starting and running a business, bringing in trainers to teach interested people how to make shoes. Alice was one of the church members invited to learn the craft of shoemaking and acquire business skills to sell them for a profit. She accepted the offer and worked diligently to learn everything she could. She quickly discovered that she enjoyed making and repairing shoes and was a natural at it. Within a short time, she was able to move her family to a nicer house in a better part of Kibera. She now sees a brighter future for herself and her children. She's confident she can provide for them and prays they will have a better life than she has endured.

"I have two sons," says Alice. "One wants to be an engineer and the other wants to be a doctor." These are dreams that she wants to help them fulfill.

The shoe project has continued, equipping many other church members with skills that immediately transfer into income-generating programs. After LIA's three-year engagement ended and full leadership of this and other development programs in Kibera was passed to the local churches, the transformation continued throughout the community and expanded to areas surrounding Kibera as well.

The shoemakers decided to specialize in different parts of the process where they excelled—cutting, gluing, beadwork, and selling. This division of labor improved the quality of the product, allowed them to produce more shoes, and helped them market and sell them more efficiently. They have now increased their product line, learning how to make jewelry and handbags, too. The income generated has improved the lives of everyone involved.

Shosh, who specializes in selling shoes, says, "I had just about given up, but now I have joy and hope in my life!"

Pastor Michael says the ripple effect continues. The partnership has decided to hire a full-time coordinator to manage the programs. This coordinator is paid through the partnership and through a contribution from the LIA medical and dental clinic that was set up in Kibera. Additional community health educators have been trained and are serving passionately. Their work continues, even though LIA is no longer in a training role.

These educators have learned to recognize the signs of common diseases, such as pneumonia, malaria, and tuberculosis, and they help people get the right medicine. They have also reduced the disease rates by improving hygiene in the community. As one transformational development agent explained, "I am able to educate people how to live well, how to eat well, and how to see the way of cleanliness. There is a lot of change in our community."

HIV/AIDS is still a huge problem in Kibera, and the social stigma is such that people often stay hidden in their small homes and don't go to the hospital for diagnosis or treatment. Many are bedridden and have no money. Health workers from local churches who are trained by LIA began going door-to-door to provide support for people living with HIV/AIDS. They cared for people and prayed for them, brought them to the clinic to get medicine, took them to support groups, and encouraged them to "live positively." The community educators now say there is greater awareness and less stigma regarding HIV/AIDS in Kibera. They are also working to prevent transmission of HIV, especially among young pregnant women.

Pastor Michael says the training of trainers and the cohesive church partnerships in Kibera have served not only to bring the denominations together, but have also had the ancillary result of diminishing tribalism. For himself and many others, he says, "This is miraculous work that has never been done before with any other organizations working in Kibera."

Questions for Reflection and Journaling:

1. How does your heart respond to the stories in this chapter? What sorts of ideas do they stir in you?

2. Where do you see opportunities in your own surroundings to bring hope to the hopeless?

3. What fruit do you see in your own life and ministry right now? Is it fruit that will last?

4. What is God calling you to get involved in right now? Ask him, listen, and respond.

24

IMPACT ASSESSMENT STUDY

*We need to regularly stop and take stock; to sit down and determine
within ourselves which things are worth valuing and which things
are not; which risks are worth the cost and which are not.*
EPICTETUS

*Let another praise you, and not your own mouth;
a stranger, and not your own lips.*
PROVERBS 27:2

FLORENCE

When I speak with church missions boards or foundations about
the work of Life In Abundance, the stories you've just read provide
examples of the wonderful fruit we've seen in recent years in many
different parts of the world. But while they are captured by the stories, as businesspeople they would always like to see documented
proof of outcomes. We've learned that data is important, and it needs
to be the right kind of data—showing not only activity, but also
impact.

For many years, we have had anecdotal evidence of our programs'
long-term success in communities where we have partnered, but some
of the Christian foundations that supported our work requested
objective data showing the sustainability of our programs.

In 2015, we invited an outside group, the Institute for Urban

Initiatives, to study the lasting effects of our model of transformational development. The researchers' conclusions were clear: "The community work established by LIA continues to flourish even after LIA is no longer present. In all the sites we visited, there is no question that the people are engaged in effective and transformative ways to bring change to their communities."[1]

We hope you gain further insight into the fruit that comes from applying the principles of transformational development as you read a very abridged version of the study's executive summary below.[2]

WHEN FAITH INTERSECTS WITH DEVELOPMENT

Searching for Sustainable Impact in the Community Work of Life In Abundance International

Methodology

The Institute for Urban Initiatives selected six program sites to study, three in Kenya and three in Ethiopia, countries where LIA has been at work for a long time and that are politically open to Christian and missionary activity.

The criteria for selection were as follows:

1. LIA was no longer working at these sites.
2. There were distinct types of projects within each site.
3. There was a mixture of urban slums and rural centers of poverty in order to determine whether the model was effective in both settings.

Multiple interviews and focus groups were conducted in each community. After gathering the data, the community researchers came together for data analysis with the Urban Initiatives team. The researchers used two frameworks to evaluate the data.

First, they looked at the aspects of economic empowerment,

community health, education, social engagement, spiritual transformation, and the programs' impact on the environment. This analysis enabled them to evaluate the program areas in which sustainable transformation occurred at each of the six sites.

Second, a model was developed to understand the level of transformation achieved at each of the sites. This analysis assessed the following factors:

- Whether beneficiaries who participated in the program gained skills and accessed resources that enabled them to continue to transform their lives after completion of the program
- Whether this transformation spread beyond the lives of the beneficiaries to have a positive impact on others in the community and whether this impact occurred on an ongoing basis
- Whether the community developed the capacity to sustain transformational development programs after LIA completed its work, thus replicating the program's benefits

Findings

Economic Empowerment

Across all six sites in the study, the researchers found that when financial security was achieved, the quality of life both at the individual level and at the community level was greatly improved. People received training and education in how to run a business, how to establish and manage a table bank, and how to build the capacity to establish financial security in their homes. Seed money, in combination with this training, resulted in multiple projects that restored dignity and confidence in communities once overwhelmed by poverty.

At all six research sites, the lives of program participants were fundamentally transformed through participation in income-generating programs. Microloans and savings plans had a significant impact.

Since the end of LIA's active involvement, recipients of microloans are giving loans to their neighbors or helping them get loans through the table bank. Thus, a ripple effect throughout the community has been created.

Community Health

The research shows the phenomenal impact that church volunteers can have on the health of a community. Trained with basic health skills and knowledge, and possessing a spirit of service obtained through spiritual teaching, these transformational development agents (TDAs) were empowered to care for their families and friends, and they were trained to teach others to do the same. Across all six sites, the TDAs remained active after LIA's departure, working to improve the health of their communities. The energy and effectiveness of the TDAs were sustainable, and also contagious.

At all six sites, community members reported that the health benefits achieved during the time of the LIA program were continued, and in some cases had been expanded since LIA's departure. Significant ongoing reductions in infectious diseases—particularly diarrhea, tuberculosis, and malaria—as well as reductions in transmission of HIV and improvements in HIV/AIDS patient care, were reported.

Education

Education provides the basis for transformational development and occurs at multiple levels throughout LIA's wholistic development model. In fact, education is embedded within each of LIA's program areas, and LIA has played a critical role in furthering formal education, including enrollment in primary and secondary schools, as well as vocational training programs.

At all six sites, researchers found that LIA's focus on education was the fuel that allowed transformation to occur and continue. It enabled the cycle of poverty to be broken. Moreover, education, by its very nature, is sustainable. Once people have developed skills, knowledge, and an empowered mindset, they have these capabilities to draw upon throughout their lives, as well as the ability to teach these same skills to others.

Environmental Transformation

At all six sites, positive and sustainable environmental impact was clearly present. Systems for rubbish and human waste disposal that were critical to improving health and quality of life were still in place, well maintained, and in many cases improved. The LIA programs also included an emphasis on beautifying the environment through tree planting, recycling, and environmental education.

Social Engagement

Mobilizing communities to take ownership, demonstrate leadership, and work toward systematic change in their communities is essential to long-term transformation. Across all six sites, researchers saw many examples of social engagement within the communities. LIA helped to equip communities to represent and protect themselves from oppressive systems. They encouraged partner churches to use their unique position in the community to give voice to the most vulnerable. LIA trained local leaders and built community capacity as a core strategy for achieving long-term sustainability. LIA leadership training begins with pastors and religious leaders, and it also reaches out to community, youth, civic, and government leaders. This strategy of mobilizing the community and equipping leaders to carry out transformational development was evident at all six sites.

Across all sites, project participants explained how LIA taught them to simultaneously work and pray for their communities. As members of the community initiated new programs, structural changes often followed.

Women across all sites told researchers repeatedly that before the

LIA project, they were just sitting, waiting for help. After learning income-generating and health-care skills, the women became more active members in the economic and social fabric of their communities. One woman participant stated, "Before, we just stayed home and waited for our husbands or friends to come at night carrying everything. But after we were taught these skills, we knew we could produce for our families. So from that time on, we've known how to work with our own hands, start small businesses, and make things— we make and save money!"

Spiritual Transformation

Interwoven into the education and training that LIA brings to a community is a deep sense of dependence on God. For LIA staff, God alone deserves the credit for everything that is accomplished. This is further emphasized by a model that brings together churches as the core institutions within the community. These local churches then learn to embrace and partner with other local institutions, businesses, and groups. Across all six sites, researchers found evidence of spiritual transformation among pastors in their approach toward leading their congregations and serving their communities, as well as among the beneficiaries and their families.

Spiritual transformation is the heart of LIA's development model, as it provides people with the hope, passion, and determination to create long-standing change within their lives and their communities. Development becomes transformational development when the spiritual aspect is in place. As peoples' hearts and minds are transformed, the impact is irreversible.

Prayer is at the core of all that LIA does. In every community, researchers observed people praying in meetings and talking about the effect of prayer on what they had done and continued to do. Every deed of kindness, every act of compassion, every skill utilized is seen as the result of a prayerful, changed life.

Across all six sites, participants said there was more harmony in their households as a result of LIA's spiritual teaching. In addition, participants at every site noted that as they experienced spiritual transformation, they also experienced psychological transformation, breaking them out of a lifestyle of dependence and freeing them to take ownership of creating change in their lives.

Levels of Sustainability

In order to understand the depth of sustainability achieved during LIA's three-year engagements, researchers used a second framework to evaluate the level of transformation achieved within each community. Transformational development, according to the LIA model, occurs within individuals, families, and communities, with strong interaction between each of these levels. With this second phase of analysis, researchers addressed three critical questions:

1. Did program participants gain skills and access resources enabling them to continue to transform their lives after completion of the LIA program?
2. Did this transformation spread beyond the lives of the participants to have a positive impact on their families and others in the community, and did this impact occur on an ongoing basis?
3. Was the capacity developed to sustain the programs once they were established and replicate the benefits throughout the community and to surrounding communities?

LEVEL 1: PROGRAM PARTICIPANTS

At all six sites, researchers met many participants whose lives had been sustainably transformed through participation in the LIA programs. Achieving sustainability at this level involves acquiring skills and accessing resources that continue to be utilized to achieve ongoing growth and transformation after the LIA involvement is complete.

LEVEL 2: FAMILY AND COMMUNITY

In every community, researchers found significant impact in each area of the development model: communities were healthier, economic activity increased, environments were cleaner, and lives were transformed by God's presence and healing. Participants explained over and over how transformation in their own lives led to transformation in their families and also empowered them to reach out and serve their neighbors. As this positive impact spread, the community became empowered with skills and resources, just like the individual participants, to carry out the work at the community level. In fact, in many cases, researchers found that the ripple effect of impact within the community actually increased over time rather than remaining constant or fading out.

LEVEL 3: COMMUNITY PROGRAM REPLICATION

The strongest level of sustainability was seen when communities developed enough capacity to carry out transformational development programs on their own. The community may take ownership of the program initially started in partnership with LIA or it may choose to initiate other transformational development projects, with the key factor being that the work is entirely community-led. At this level of sustainability, program benefits are replicated over and over, creating a movement toward achieving greater widespread transformation. In at least three of the six sites, the community is carrying out the programs initiated in partnership with LIA.

Conclusion

The overall conclusions of the outside investigative team of researchers are clear: The community work established by LIA continued to flourish even after LIA was no longer present. At every site researchers visited, there was no question that the people continued to be engaged in effective and transformative ways to bring change to their communities through the local churches. Over and over, researchers heard participants say, "Our eyes have been opened." Having learned the effectiveness of working together, they gained the capacity and skills to think creatively about the challenges they faced, and they agreed there would be no turning back. A *change in mindset* was the key result. Most people interviewed were excited and passionate about the differences they had seen, especially when they were able to overcome long-standing difficulties by utilizing new skills that they had learned through the program.

At each of the six study sites, researchers saw that communities continued to seek ways to improve their health and vitality, to learn new skills and gain knowledge, to use those skills to increase their incomes, and to care deeply for one another, long after LIA had gone. And beyond those benefits, they demonstrated to the broader community that by working together (churches, businesses, and neighborhoods), they did not have to wait for someone to save them, but they could become the agents of their own transformation.

In the opinion of the researchers, LIA has accomplished a tremendous amount of work with limited funds. Central to LIA's philosophy is the conviction that money is not the answer to a community's problems. *Education, skills, taking ownership*, and *working together* are what create lasting change. LIA adheres to its own principles, using a small amount of money to generate change that is replicable and sustainable into the future.

To achieve this transformational change, a wholistic model of development is essential.

The components of LIA's development model are all vitally important and work together to achieve success. The interdependencies were evident across all research sites, with the local church taking the lead role. Spiritual transformation is the seed that ignites change, and it is also the mechanism by which the work is carried on into the future. Local church congregations provide a body of volunteers who are willing to serve their community—passionately and compassionately—and take ownership for continuing the transformation process.

Questions for Reflection and Journaling

1. What would an independent research company report if they visited your ministry?

2. How would you feel if someone wanted to review, study, or audit your life or ministry?

3. When you hear praise about you or your organization's work, how do you respond, and to what do you attribute your success?

PART 4

HOW THIS AFFECTS *YOU*

THE NEW MISSIONS LANDSCAPE

Admit that the waters
Around you have grown
And accept it that soon
You'll be drenched to the bone . . .
For the times they are a-changin'
BOB DYLAN

Behold, I am doing a new thing; now it springs forth, do you not
perceive it? I will make a way in the wilderness and rivers in the desert.
ISAIAH 43:19

FLORENCE AND CHARLIE

We have been sharing our hearts as two disciples and disciple-makers, reporting to you what we have found to be currently bearing lasting fruit and receiving God's blessing. One thing we have observed is that the global missions field is experiencing major changes and challenges—especially in large urban settings—making strategic partnerships even more important.

The times and seasons belong to God.[1] He knows we live in a world of constant uncertainty, with pandemics, economic downturns, wars, open borders, closed countries, persecution, and so many other variables. Yes, our ministry circumstances change, but God never changes. That being said, we have entered a new season of missions, and the entire landscape is different.

The Christian World Map Is Being Redrawn

Since the close of the twentieth century, a dramatic shift has occurred in the demographics of the Christian world. Throughout modern history, the Global North (with the rich and powerful regions of North America and Europe) has been home to the majority of Christians in the world. But now that designation has moved to the Global South (the traditionally poorer regions of South America, Africa, and Asia).

The following statistics show the movement of this global shift:

- In 1900, only 18 percent of all Christians lived in the Global South, while 82 percent lived in the Global North.
- By 2020, fully 66 percent of all Christians lived in the Global South, while only 33 percent lived in the Global North.
- By 2050, it is projected that 77 percent of all Christians will live in the Global South, with only 23 percent in the Global North.[2]

One key aspect of this shift is a gradual decline of Christianity in the Global North, which is being outpaced by the boom in Christianity in the Global South. Because this boom is happening faster than the decline, the number of Christians worldwide is showing rapid growth, even as the influence of Christianity fades in the Global North.

For example, over the last fifteen years, the number of adults who identify as Christians in the United States has dropped from 78 to 63 percent.[3] If that trend continues, Christians could make up less than half the US population by the year 2070.[4]

According to a 2019 study by the Pew Center, "If demography is destiny, then Christianity's future lies in Africa. By 2060, a plurality of Christians—more than four-in-ten—will call sub-Saharan Africa home, up from 26 percent in 2015."[5]

In 1910, there were two million Christians in Africa. Today there are 650 million, with an estimated 200 million evangelicals.[6] This is indeed a potential mission force arising from what was clearly a mission field only a few decades ago—and already the Global South has been actively sending out missionaries.

An honest awareness of this tectonic shift demands an adjustment in our approach to missions in the Global North and West. We need a fresh mindset about who is called to go as cross-cultural missionaries and who is called to send them. These statistics help inform us about the way partnerships work in this new context.

God is not surprised by these numbers! He knew this would happen, and he had this plan in mind when he called us—all of us—to go make disciples of all nations.

How Can We Adapt to These Global Changes?

The time has come for us to ask how these changes and shifts affect our current missions approach. We believe it is wise to respond soberly, but also not miss the chance to take advantage of emerging new opportunities to fully engage.

First of all, the church needs to see these changes as an opportunity for partnerships. The growth of the church across Africa will reshape and eventually transform the face of Christianity globally. This presents an opportunity for the Global North to intentionally engage in this rapid growth to help it spread widely throughout the African continent and beyond.

That engagement will happen best through North/South partnerships with indigenous organizations and independent churches in these countries.

"From the West to the Rest" is no longer the prevailing model. Nations that were once the mission field are now sending out waves of new missionaries. It is their season to serve, rather than waiting to be served. They need to take the initiative, seeing themselves as contributors and initiators, not just recipients; equipped and chosen to serve, not weak and needy.

Indigenous leaders in the Global South are positioned and

culturally equipped to fulfill integral wholistic missions in their own communities, countries, and continents. They have an opportunity to make the most of this changing landscape by forming partnerships with leaders in the Global North to augment their capacity and strengthen areas that could be improved for exponential growth and impact. Together we have the opportunity to be part of something bigger than our current efforts by joining God in what he is already doing.

That said, these new partnerships must be entered into with great discernment. Partner relationships must be built on trust and mutual submission—not like business relationships based on contracts and transactions. The invitation is to seek, steward, and grow Spirit-led partnerships that result from focused time in prayer and following God's lead.

If we pursue these God-birthed partnerships, operating in unity as equals, the world will take notice that we are God's people, disciples of Jesus, loving each other and the communities we serve. God-honoring partners have an innate desire to grow and advance the Kingdom of God, not work selfishly to build and develop their own brand, name, or influence. Paul tells us to "love one another with brotherly affection. Outdo one another in showing honor."[7] That's great advice for working together with cross-cultural partners: Try to outdo each other in showing love and honor!

The new landscape demands that we intentionally place the local church at the forefront of our efforts so that the community will center its attention on the bride of Christ—and ultimately on Christ himself.

As South and North partner together, go together, and serve together, we must be on the same page with one another in our practices and strategies, to be certain we are upholding the dignity of those we serve. Our projects must be customized to fit those we are intending to help, ensuring that they have the resources and capabilities to sustain those efforts on their own. Otherwise we're only building or perpetuating their dependence.

As our partnerships work together in a community, it is vitally important to identify local capacities and work to expand them so that the community will realize just how much they can do on their own. Once they truly grasp how much they are capable of doing for themselves, they can begin to actively participate in the development of their community.

It may seem easier and faster to go it alone, but true partnerships are beautiful in the sight of God and command his blessing. As we enter these partnerships, he promises to go with us.

It's Time to Evaluate and Change Strategy

Another appropriate response to the shifting missions landscape is seeing it as an opportunity to change strategy. The history of world missions teaches us that major changes in strategy have already happened on a global scale at least three times.

The First Era: To the Coastlands

William Carey, often called the Father of Modern Missions, was inspired by the invention of the mariner's compass. Carey realized this strategic new tool opened new doors for sailing to distant lands to reach their inhabitants.[8] Under his influence, the focus of missions strategy shifted to distant shores, as the coastlands of the world's continents became the mission field of the late eighteenth to early twentieth century.

The Second Era: To the Interior

In the mid-nineteenth century, missionaries such as David Livingstone and Hudson Taylor lamented the growing mission compounds, fenced off from the people they were intended to serve, and they led a movement into the often unknown and unexplored regions further inland. The missionaries of this era ventured past the coastlands and reached the interior of continents with the gospel.

The Third Era: To Every People Group

In the mid-twentieth century, missiologists—including Cameron Townsend, Donald McGavran, Ralph Winter, and others—recognized that the task was not solely defined by geographical or political boundaries, but by people groups—thousands of whom were yet unreached. This expansion of the missions task led to multiple organizations rethinking their outreach strategies to focus on those throughout the world who had not yet heard the good news.

It's important to note that the dawn of each new era did not displace the previous ones. Missionaries still serve on the coastlands today, just as in Carey's era. There are still vital groundbreaking ministries working in the interior of continents. And there are still many people groups that do not have a church in their own culture.

Whether the changes we're seeing are signaling the arrival of a new era in missions, we're not sure. But it's clear that many of our existing strategies and methods need to be reevaluated and perhaps changed. This becomes clear when we look at how world missions was done only a generation ago.

Then, mission agencies operated in silos or separate departments—such as medical missions, translation work, or church planting. Medical care focused primarily on curative approaches—treating and healing diseases. Their clinics or hospitals were set up in institutions. Missionaries went to the field as long-term career missionaries, sent by mission agencies from the West (or what we now call the Global North).

That was fine—at the time, it seemed to work—and we didn't know any better. This strategy has gotten us to where we are today, and we stand on the shoulders of our church fathers and mothers. Their sacrifice, faithfulness, and perseverance have created a huge army around the world, Christ's church, ready and poised to enter this mission God has given us. God is simply calling us to a new paradigm—though not new to him; it has always been the way outlined through his Word.

Those who operated in that siloed system lived with many

disadvantages (perhaps without realizing they were disadvantages). These included creating dependency, undermining people's dignity, lacking local ownership, and limiting what the vision-bearers could handle before they burned out.

That model has a history to overcome. It is equivalent to a political superpower creating a colony. It reeks of the boss-and-servant mentality. It arrives with authority and expertise rather than a servant's heart. The missions group decides what the local receiving population needs, doles it out, promotes their generosity to their senders back home, and grows stronger.

Anyone can now see the obvious problems in that model, but it isn't an easy paradigm to break, because it gives the ones in charge some distinct advantages. They have ownership, security, and status. They feel needed, receive the credit, and are looked up to as heroes.

But mission fields have changed. Indigenous churches and mission agencies are sending missionaries from what was previously seen as the mission field. Community-based organizations have been set up in large numbers and have made inroads. Churches have been planted. For the most part, even in closed countries, national Christians who speak the language of the target people group (and also speak English) can be identified, mobilized, and equipped to work in places that are difficult or impossible for a foreigner to enter.

Technology has advanced, and communication tools have grown more powerful and more mobile. The gospel is made available in new and innovative ways. Even denominational lines of division are weakening and dying.

It's Time to Embrace Change

In times of transition, it helps to examine what is already working. Based on our interactions with ministries throughout Africa, South America, Asia, and the Middle East, we can report that transformational strategies growing from unified cross-cultural partnerships are the ones that are producing lasting fruit.

Just as going it alone is often easier than working in partnership with others, it's also easier to stick to what we know and keep doing what we've always done. If that sounds like you or your organization, here's some bad news: If you don't like to embrace change, you'll probably dislike becoming irrelevant even more!

When God moves, as his disciples we must follow. Sometimes that means we have to take a long, hard look at how the changes affect us, and then, through much prayer and seeking God's wisdom and guidance, determine what needs to change in how we're operating. Then we need to take the opportunity to reset and quickly realign ourselves with what God is doing.

We can respond to the shifts and changes that are happening globally by seeing them as an opportunity to seek God's guidance, trusting that what will emerge is something more sustainable, more equitable, and more glorifying to God and his Church.

Do These Changes Affect Your Assignment?

The shifting missions landscape may also be an opportunity to reassess your personal calling. We are all still commissioned to go and make disciples of all nations. But *how* we do it may be up for review. This may be an appropriate time to reappraise what God is doing and how he is inviting you to partner with him.

As we discussed previously, that appraisal involves inspecting the fruit of our lives and our ministries. And we have to be honest. If the fruit we are producing is of poor quality or the harvest is small, it's time to own up to that reality and seek God's direction.

You have an opportunity right now to review your personal calling so that you can allow God to cut off the dead or unproductive parts of what you are doing in your service for him. Then, with the remaining branches that *are* bearing fruit, allow God to prune them and shore them up so they will produce more and better fruit.

Maintaining the status quo isn't good enough. What always

seemed to work in the past probably isn't working nearly as well anymore. It's time for reassessment, change, and new growth.

We are all identified by many labels.

I, Charlie, am a pastor, dentist, businessman, husband, and father.

I, Florence, am a doctor, wife, mother, university chancellor, and ministry founder.

You also have many labels, but as Christians, our first and foremost identifier must be that we are disciples of Jesus Christ.

We are at a defining moment in the history of the world. We must respond as disciples of Jesus on a mission to make more disciples. It's time for new partnerships. It's time to review our current strategies and allow them to inform our calling. To be willing to be spent means giving ourselves away in service, with a surrendered posture—applied at the level of the recipient—to see God's Kingdom come. "It is no longer I who live, but Christ who lives in me."[9] The people who do ministry from a top-down perspective give of their skills, time, and resources. But there is a level at which we also give of *ourselves* and allow ourselves to be spent for those we serve.

Without a doubt, it is costly to give our lives to ministry. It seems easier to hold on to power and authority and do all the work yourself. But think of how Jesus ministered: He transformed his disciples into trusted coworkers in just three years. He delegated, empowered, and gave them real authority—even the authority to cast out demons. Those are rather high-profile skills to place in the hands of trainees!

Jesus taught them what they needed to know and do to be effective. Then he sent them out to do ministry, and they reported their results to him. This allowed them to learn from their mistakes and failures. Then, before they thought they were ready, he handed the whole ministry over to them. After telling them to go to the nations and do as he had taught them, he phased out of direct ministry—but he left his disciples with the same powerful resource for wisdom, guidance, and direction that he had during his time on earth; namely, his Holy Spirit.

Jesus came to bring life—his abundant life. He did not come

merely to serve, for that would have sharply curtailed the effectiveness of his ministry. His role was to demonstrate, train, empower, and step back to facilitate the establishment of his Father's Kingdom on earth.

This step-back/phase-out process is difficult for many leaders. Even after practicing these principles for many years in the mission field, it still feels to both of us like we are taking baby steps in this regard. However, we are determined to give fully of ourselves in surrender to God's will rather than operate from a safe place of merely rendering our skills and resources.

May the Lord bless you to that end as well.

Questions for Reflection and Journaling

1. What new thoughts do the statistics in this chapter spark in your mind?

2. What cross-cultural partnerships are you actively pursuing with organizations and other Christians?

3. Are you ready to embrace change and open your mind to new strategies and methods that God may show you? Won't you stop and pray right now and ask him for his direction for your future ministry?

SHAPING A KINGDOM MINDSET

Be assured, if you walk with Him and look to Him, and
expect help from Him, He will never fail you.
GEORGE MÜLLER

Finally, then, brothers, we ask and urge you in the Lord Jesus,
that as you received from us how you ought to walk and to please
God, just as you are doing, that you do so more and more.
1 THESSALONIANS 4:1

FLORENCE

I was planning an important trip from the United States, where my family was temporarily based, to visit one of our sites in a rather unsafe closed country. As the days passed and the time of my departure neared, the thought became clearer and stronger in my mind that I might die on this trip. I actually became quite certain I would not survive, and yet I knew I was still supposed to go—I did not feel any liberty to cancel the trip. It became so clear during my final days of packing that I decided to copy my legal papers and travel documents and leave them in a place where Festus could easily find them.

I obediently boarded the plane with a deep sense of eternity in my heart. Ten hours later, the plane landed in Amsterdam, where I had a layover before boarding my next flight. I spent that first flight seeking God, and by the time I arrived at Schiphol Airport, I was completely broken and willing to lay down my life, if that was God's plan for me. I even began to sense that the next connecting flight might be when my life would end, and I concluded that I should call the team I was on my way to visit, to let them know that, even if I didn't make it, their mission was still vital and they must proceed without me.

The Amsterdam airport was busy, so I went in search of a quiet place to find some solitude. I came upon a secluded area upstairs and entered a restroom. Since it was still very early in the morning, I thought I could spend some time alone, pouring out my heart to God and getting ready to meet him face-to-face.

When I walked into the restroom, I was disappointed to find a woman already in there, brushing her hair. As I entered, it was obvious she was equally surprised to see me. She stopped brushing her hair and stared at me uncomfortably. I mumbled a greeting and walked into a stall. When I came out a short time later, she was still there. She had put away her brush and was standing by the sinks, waiting for me.

She asked if I was a medical doctor. As I answered, I looked at her closely, wondering whether we had met somewhere before. Then she asked if I was in ministry. I confirmed that I was. At this, her face brightened, and she excitedly began to tell me why it was that she had come to this out-of-the-way restroom at this particular time.

She was from Washington, DC, and was returning home from a United Nations trip to Tanzania. She did not know me, yet God had impressed on her to pray specifically for me for the entire previous week. He told her that during her layover in Amsterdam, she was to find this exact restroom where she would meet me and pray with me. At that moment I was quite certain that my time to leave this earth must be imminent, that God had sent her to prepare me.

The rest of our time together was beyond wonderful! We prayed together and she shared with me several prophetic messages. She told me I was not to fear, for this mission was not unto death. She assured me that I would be returning home through Amsterdam, and that the work prepared for me to do was not yet complete. Then, far too soon, she gave me her business card and ran off to catch her connecting flight home.

A week later, when I went back through Amsterdam, I stopped at that same restroom to thank God for his protection and faithfulness. As a matter of fact, whenever I pass through Schiphol Airport now, I make a point to go to that restroom and thank God that he has kept me alive for his purpose.

If that woman hadn't given me her business card, I very likely would have thought I had met an angel. But she is a real person, a professor in pediatrics and an associate pastor serving in a church near Washington, DC.

After a short time of private praise to God, I boarded my onward flight with a renewed sense of purpose, assured of my Father's great love and his hand of protection over my life and the work he has called me to.

But I was also reminded that we are to live always with an eternal perspective, ready to lay down our lives for the Kingdom of God. We must continually die to ourselves in our service of the King of kings. Jesus made it clear, "If anyone would come after me, let him deny himself and take up his cross daily and follow me."[1]

Self-Sacrifice Is Nonnegotiable

Death to self is the initial and requisite step to discipleship. If we do not take up our cross *daily*, we cannot be Christ's disciples. Because only those who have been discipled themselves can disciple others, we cannot make other disciples for Jesus unless we have died to ourselves and are sold out to him. This is not a popular strategy you'll hear in missions books or at conventions, but it's God's strategy for us: Deny yourself and crucify your selfish ambitions; then you can bring forth lasting fruit of eternal value.

I remember the night when I first sacrificed myself to him and took up my cross. It was November 19, 1981. It was an unmistakable turning point.

I had been questioning God on the purpose of my life. I had lost my father tragically—and he had always been my hero and my motivation for pursuing success. That night, as I sought the Lord to reveal to me what life was really all about, why I had been created, and what I was to accomplish before I died, he revealed to me that I was created for worship and he was the author of what form that worship would take. As such, my part was to allow him to own me and fulfill his pleasing and perfect will in me.

I had accepted Jesus as my Savior several years earlier and had given him my heart. But that night I gave him my entire life. The one I had known as Savior also became my Lord. For the first time, I truly became a disciple and entered into a lifelong covenant with Christ, giving him full control and ownership of my dreams, my future, my everything—allowing him to use me however and wherever he desired, for his glory.

From that night, it was no longer Florence who lived, but Christ who lived in me.[2] It changed my entire outlook on my life and ministry. I pray that you, too, know the freedom of complete surrender to God.

Death Is Necessary for a Harvest

In John 12:24, Jesus gives the example of a kernel of wheat: Unless it falls into the ground and dies, it remains only a single seed. But if it dies, it produces a harvest containing countless seeds. No death means no fruit . . . at least not the kind that lasts.

Through death we are transformed, from one state of existence to another. And transformed people, in partnership with God, can facilitate transformation in others. But first we must come to the end of ourselves.

What does "death to self" do in our lives? One thing I've learned is that it replaces our unhealthy motivations for serving God. It's so easy to seek more of the feelings we get from serving, rather than pursuing God himself. When we come to a place where those self-focused feelings are taken away, we learn to love God for who he is and what he wants to do in the world, not for what we can do for him or get from him.

When someone talks about something you did, but they mess up the facts and give credit to someone else, is that okay with you? Can you leave it be, without trying to get the credit or without harboring resentment in your heart? When we no longer keep a list of what we have achieved, when we no longer care who gets the credit, when we rejoice at the success of others, then we have some evidence that we are denying ourselves in following Jesus.

Jesus tells us in Luke 9:23 that we are to take up our cross daily. Truthfully, some days I sadly realize that another piece of me still needs to be crucified. But I have come to understand that unless I become totally dead to myself, I cannot be totally alive to Christ. It is a matter of daily prayer, because some of the things we have already crucified are very capable of resurrecting themselves in our lives. For true disciples and disciple-makers—those of us who give our lives to Christ, not just our service—daily dying to self becomes an important, ongoing lifestyle.

Don't Miss God's Plan for Your Life

If the 1999 Christmas Eve incident had not confounded me and driven me to depend on the local church, I would probably still be very busy in that first community in Ethiopia, doing good work among a relatively small group of people, being seen as the hero and doing things *for* people and *to* people. Likely burnt out, yet feeling indispensable and creating dependency. Doing good, but demeaning the bride of Christ, and in the process, actually doing harm.

I want to point out that God has a plan for you, and he has already set things aside that he specifically wants you to do. Scripture tells us, "We are his workmanship, created in Christ Jesus for good works, which God prepared beforehand, that we should walk in them."[3] There are things that you are uniquely gifted to do for him. But they require preparation—*being* before *doing*, always—and sacrificing your goals, dreams, and self in order to follow him.

God does not call people to become heroes and gain glory. He calls us to die to ourselves and exalt *him*. It is by equipping the local church, empowering the people there to continue bringing transformation to their communities, that we can make an impact—a sustained impact—in the work we are called to do.

I am amazed, but not surprised, at how abundantly God blesses this strategy. As we have sought him over the years, he has shown us how sustainable development can be achieved. It was his way all along.

When Isaiah prophesies Jesus' mission in Isaiah 61:11, he concludes by saying, "For as the earth brings forth its sprouts, and as a garden causes what is sown in it to sprout up, so the Lord GOD will cause righteousness and praise to sprout up before all the nations."

There is no sprouting, no new growth, and no harvest unless the seed first goes into the ground and dies. Isaiah foretold that the fruits of righteousness and praise would be a harvest in the nations.

The World Needs Wholistic Ministry

Today there is a huge open door of opportunity in front of us. You will see it wherever the poor can be found. They are very receptive to the gospel, the good news of Jesus, especially if it is presented in a wholistic way that shows we care for and love them—the whole person.

Remember Jesus' words in Matthew 25:34-40:

The King will say to those on his right, . . . "For I was hungry and you gave me food, I was thirsty and you gave me drink, I was a stranger and you welcomed me, I was naked and you clothed me, I was sick and you visited me, I was in prison and you came to me." Then the righteous will answer him, saying, "Lord, when did we see you hungry and feed you, or thirsty and give you drink? And when did we see you a stranger and welcome you, or naked and clothe you? And when did we see you sick or in prison and visit you?" And the King will answer them, "Truly, I say to you, as you did it to one of the least of these my brothers, you did it to me."

This passage shows that Jesus saw the gospel from a wholistic viewpoint. This should have been no surprise to the first-century audience Jesus was speaking to, because the wholistic style of ministry was predicted by the prophet Isaiah:

The Spirit of the Lord God is upon me,
> because the Lord has anointed me
to bring good news to the poor;
> he has sent me to bind up the brokenhearted,
to proclaim liberty to the captives,
> and the opening of the prison to those who are bound;
to proclaim the year of the Lord's favor,
> and the day of vengeance of our God;
to comfort all who mourn;
to grant to those who mourn in Zion—
> to give them a beautiful headdress instead of ashes,
the oil of gladness instead of mourning,
> the garment of praise instead of a faint spirit;
that they may be called oaks of righteousness,
> the planting of the Lord, that he may be glorified.

ISAIAH 61:1-3

The biggest hindrance to accomplishing God's mission today is those people who are busy doing ministry activities without spending time *being* with the Lord to know what he wants done and how to do it.

We have each been called to serve God in a unique way. There are specific plans set by our Creator. If you do not know how or where he is calling you to serve, start seeking him with all your heart and listening for his voice.

As you do this, here are some other principles to keep in mind.

We Must Have a Transformed Mindset

In order to serve God well, we need a transformed mindset. The apostle Paul talks about this in his letters to the churches in the New Testament.

> Let this mind be in you, which also was in Christ Jesus.
> PHILIPPIANS 2:5 (KJV)

> The natural person does not accept the things of the Spirit of God, for they are folly to him, and he is not able to understand them because they are spiritually discerned. . . . "For who has understood the mind of the Lord so as to instruct him?" But we have the mind of Christ.
> 1 CORINTHIANS 2:14, 16

> Present your bodies as a living sacrifice, holy and acceptable to God, which is your spiritual worship. Do not be conformed to this world, but be transformed by the renewal of your mind, that by testing you may discern what is the will of God, what is good and acceptable and perfect.
> ROMANS 12:1-2

This renewal of our minds results in an eternal perspective, so that we take our eyes and our focus off the things of this world and instead prioritize what will last for eternity.

Do not lay up for yourselves treasures on earth, where moth and rust destroy and where thieves break in and steal, but lay up for yourselves treasures in heaven, where neither moth nor rust destroys and where thieves do not break in and steal. For where your treasure is, there your heart will be also.

MATTHEW 6:19-21

Full Surrender Is a Precursor to Kingdom Power

Men and women who have been willing to surrender themselves to Christ have turned the world upside down. In their weakness, Kingdom power was manifested. Why are we not making a greater impact today? Look at what people of the early church did as ministry, then look at what we call ministry today. Many get into "God's work" with great care not to get their hands dirty. But God asks us to jump into his service with both feet.

It reminds me of the response given by evangelist D. L. Moody to Henry Varley, a British revival preacher who had befriended the young Moody in Dublin and had told him, "Moody, the world has yet to see what God will do with a man fully consecrated to him."

A year later, again in conversation with Mr. Varley, Moody said,

Ah, those were the words sent to my soul, through you, from the Living God. As I crossed the wide Atlantic, the boards of the deck of the vessel were engraved with them, and when I reached Chicago, the very paving stones seemed marked with *Moody, the world has yet to see what God will do with a man fully consecrated to him.* Under the power of those words I have come back to England, and I felt that I must not let more time pass until I let you know how God had used your words to my inmost soul.[4]

I call myself to attention several times a year and remind myself before God, "I don't want *my* plan, *my* agenda, or *my* life. I want *yours*. It's not *my* house or project or family, but *your* Kingdom and *your* way." The years I served as a missionary have helped me realize that God's way of ministry means not remaining focused on *my* plans, *my* strategies, and *my* organization. It's being sensitive to what God is doing and plugging into that. We partner with *him*, not him with us.

We Need to Understand the Times We Are Living In

In Acts 14:1, Paul and Barnabas "spoke in such a way that a great number of both Jews and Greeks believed." The result is that many were added to the church. Later it says they were "speaking boldly for the Lord, who bore witness to the word of his grace, granting signs and wonders to be done by their hands."[5] Oh, I pray that would be said of us today, as well!

My friends, God is doing a significant new thing in the world at this moment. Like the men of Issachar in 1 Chronicles 12:32, we need to understand the times and know what we are to do. It's unlikely we can continue to do things the same way that we have always done them. If the results are not there, we must make changes. God's plans, done his way, will produce his harvest.

It's a monumental task, but the weight is not on our shoulders. Remember what Jesus promised: "I am with you always, to the end of the age."[6] He is with us—leading, guiding, and displaying his love through his disciples like never before. With Christ's indwelling presence, you and I can confidently obey his call to go and make disciples.

But first, there are some things we must do:

- Know whom we serve, know his voice, know his calling.
- Count the cost and die daily to ourselves.
- Become Christ's disciple, so we can disciple others.
- Choose his ways and not our own, for his glory and not our own.

- Let him transform our mindset.
- Fully surrender ourselves to him.
- Ask him to make us relevant as we bear witness for him.

If you are saying, "Yes, my Father and my God, transform me so I can serve to bring glory to you and your Kingdom," then pray with me:

Lord Jesus, today I say yes. Change the things within me that need to be changed, so I can be a clear reflection of you in this world. Disciple me, so I can make disciples of the nations. Let the old pass away—now—and let the new come in. Discard my old wineskins; renew me to carry your new wine. Create in me a new heart, a new mind, new abilities, and new gifts. Fill me with your power, your Holy Spirit. Call me, renew me, and use me in this harvest season for the task at hand.

And Lord, let me truly know you, worship you, and hear from you as never before. Help me to consciously count the cost. And having done so, help me to choose to live as your trustworthy disciple. I want to obey your call to do your will, not as a career or a vocation or a job. My Father, I choose to serve you in full surrender. I choose to listen and follow your voice, in all things and at all times.

Thank you for choosing me, for calling me, for using me. To you, my Lord, be all the glory.

In the name of Jesus Christ, my Savior, amen.

May we leave you with the admonition that Paul, along with his ministry partners Silvanus and Timothy, wrote to the believers in Thessalonica:

Finally, dear brothers and sisters, we urge you in the name of the Lord Jesus to live in a way that pleases God, as we have taught you. You live this way already, and we encourage you to do so even more.[7]

As you do, give God all the glory. You're not the hero of this story. He is.

Questions for Reflection and Journaling

1. As you've read this chapter and book, what has God been saying to you regarding your future ministry? What are the next steps you believe he wants you to take? Outline that plan in your journal or on your computer.

2. As you reflect on the stories and principles we've explained, how have they made a difference in the spiritual disciplines you practice? Are you spending more time listening to God and expecting his direction in your life?

3. Can you truly say that you've died to yourself? What signs in your life give you reassurance that you're no longer trying to be the hero?

4. Have you fully surrendered your life and future to Jesus Christ? If not, why not do it now?

5. What can you do today to start moving your life in the direction of partnering cross-culturally to see lasting transformation wherever you serve?

Contact Us

We look forward to hearing from you about how God uses this book in your life, your church, and your ministry. You may contact us at **infohq@lifeinabundance.org**.

Acknowledgments

The fruit that resulted from the principles we learned in the many communities and nations where we've worked would never have happened were it not for our spouses—Festus and Sherry—who understood that the command to "go" included us.

Our heartfelt appreciation goes out to our team at Tyndale House Publishers. Carol Traver expertly guided the project every step of the way; Dave Lindstedt deftly edited the manuscript; and designer Eva Winters captured our message and transformed it into a beautiful cover. This successful partnership came about thanks to the encouragement of Jeremy Taylor. As president of Tyndale House Foundation, he introduced the book to his colleagues, and we are grateful for his help in bringing it to a wider audience.

The writing process itself took years—interrupted by a global pandemic—with two authors based on different continents, separated by an ocean and multiple time zones. Though we had talked for years about writing a book together, it wasn't until we asked Joe and Kathy Sindorf to collaborate with us that real progress was made. Their unique combination of skills proved to be the perfect complement to our hopes for the book. They combed through thousands of pages of notes, PowerPoint slides, and conference presentations, and spent several days interviewing us in person, and many hours by Zoom, to assemble the rough content. Then they crafted an initial draft, which after several revisions became the text you now hold in your hands. We are filled with gratitude and thanks for their work unto the Lord.

We are thankful also for the skills of Onyemechalu "Stanley" Victor, who, from his home in Nigeria, quickly and precisely transcribed the many hours of interviews that provided much of the content for the book.

We wanted to have a foreword written by someone who knew us both very well and who was also well-known in the global missions world. It means so much to us that Steve Saint spent many hours reading the manuscript and providing his thoughts for the foreword.

If we were to acknowledge everyone who contributed to this book, it would take pages upon pages. Still, we want to express our deep gratitude to all our friends around the world who shaped us, and whom God used to ultimately produce this work.

Finally, we want to acknowledge you, the reader. We pray that the curiosity that led you to pick up this book will grow into an earnest desire to find your place in God's plan for the nations. And through that unity of purpose, that you will see lives, communities, and nations transformed by the power of God.

Notes

FOREWORD
1. Matthew 28:19-20, NIV.
2. 1 Corinthians 12:12, NLT.
3. Romans 10:13, NLT.
4. Romans 10:14-15, NLT.

CHAPTER 1: LET'S GO TOGETHER
1. Reginald DesRoches et al., "Overview of the 2010 Haiti Earthquake," *Earthquake Spectra* 27, no. 1 (January 1, 2011): 1–21, https://doi.org/10.1193/1.3630129.
2. Ethiopia is one of the ten nations most affected with leprosy, also known as Hansen's disease. Because leprosy is an infectious disease, its patients endure the social stigma of being considered unclean or as people who should not be associated with or touched.
3. Psalm 133:1, 3, NIV.
4. "Statistics about Life in Haiti," Restavek Freedom, accessed December 4, 2023, https://restavekfreedom.org/2017/01/20/statistics-about-life-in-haiti; "In Haiti, Access to Water and Sanitation Is Vital, and the World Bank Is Making This Possible," The World Bank, March 22, 2023, https://www.worldbank.org/en/news/feature/2023/03/22/in-haiti-access-to-water-and-sanitation-is-vital-and-the-world-bank-is-making-this-possible.
5. Maria Abi-Habib, "Why Haiti Still Despairs After $13 Billion in Foreign Aid," *New York Times*, July 8, 2021.
6. "Children in Haiti: One Year After—The Long Road from Relief to Recovery," UNICEF, January 2011, https://www.lessonsfromhaiti.org/download/Report_Center/UNICEF_Report_Children_in_Haiti_-_One_Year_After_-_The_Long_Road_from_Relief_to_Recovery_original.pdf.

CHAPTER 4: UNITED IN PRAYER IN KABUL
1. Lindsay Maizland, "The Taliban in Afghanistan," Council on Foreign Relations, updated January 19, 2023, https://www.cfr.org/backgrounder/taliban-afghanistan.
2. Maizland, "Taliban in Afghanistan."
3. The Taliban was officially out of power in Afghanistan for less than twenty years before retaking control in August 2021. Nobody knew how long the door would be open to those from the outside, so we went as soon as we could. See "A Historical Timeline of Afghanistan," PBS News Hour, May 4, 2011 (updated August 30, 2021), https://www.pbs.org/newshour/politics/asia-jan-june11-timeline-afghanistan.
4. "Afghanistan: Restricted," Voice of the Martyrs Global Prayer Guide, accessed December 5, 2023, https://www.persecution.com/globalprayerguide/afghanistan/.
5. "Afghanistan: Restricted."
6. In answer to a question we received: Yes, we have trained some women to do the dental work—depending on the setting. We ask the local church to recommend the people to be trained.

CHAPTER 5: OVERWHELMED ON CHRISTMAS EVE IN ETHIOPIA
1. Matthew 25:40.

CHAPTER 6: AN INVITATION TO A DIFFERENT WAY
1. Hippocrates, *Of the Epidemics*, book 1, sec. II, para. 5, trans. Francis Adams, accessed December 5, 2023, https://classics.mit.edu/Hippocrates/epidemics.1.i.html.
2. "Our Vision and Principles," Stand Together, accessed December 5, 2023, https://standtogether.org/about-us/.
3. Ephesians 4:4-6.

CHAPTER 7: WHAT IS TRANSFORMATIONAL DEVELOPMENT?
1. Luke 4:18-19.
2. Isaiah 61:3.
3. Isaiah 61:1-2.
4. Matthew 28:19-20.
5. Matthew 22:36-40.
6. Deuteronomy 10:18-19; Psalm 14:6; Luke 10:29-37.

CHAPTER 8: THE IMPORTANCE OF PRAYER
1. 1 Thessalonians 5:17.
2. Matthew 21:13.
3. Matthew 6:33.
4. 1 Kings 19:12.
5. Psalm 4:4.

6. Psalm 46:10.
7. Mark 1:35.

CHAPTER 9: LIVING WITH AN ETERNAL PERSPECTIVE

1. Matthew 6:21.
2. Proverbs 4:23, NIV.
3. Luke 6:45.
4. Matthew 6:26.
5. Matthew 6:32-33.
6. John 16:33.
7. John 15:18, 20.
8. 2 Corinthians 4:16-18
9. Romans 12:1-2.
10. "Global Dashboard," Joshua Project, accessed December 5, 2023, https://joshuaproject.net/people_groups/statistics.
11. Colossians 1:10.

CHAPTER 10: LOVING THE WHOLE PERSON

1. Matthew 25:35-36.
2. Luke 10:30-35, author's paraphrase.
3. Luke 10:37.

CHAPTER 11: USING RELIEF AND DEVELOPMENT WISELY

1. Galatians 6:9-10.
2. Mark 12:31.
3. John 14:12.
4. Matthew 25:35, 40.

CHAPTER 13: DON'T SEEK THE GLORY

1. Proverbs 3:5-6.
2. Matthew 5:16.
3. Isaiah 43:6-7.
4. Isaiah 42:8.

CHAPTER 14: PROGRAM OWNERSHIP BY THE LOCAL CHURCH

1. For information about the Jesus Film Project, see https://www.jesusfilm.org/.

CHAPTER 15: DISCIPLES MAKING DISCIPLES

1. "What Is the True Meaning of Christian Discipleship?," Grace Theological Seminary (blog), December 9, 2021, https://seminary.grace.edu/what-is-the -true-meaning-of-christian-discipleship.
2. Matthew 28:19-20.
3. John 1:14.
4. John 10:10.

5. Proverbs 27:17, NIV.
6. R. C. Sproul, "Developing a Passion for God," Ligonier Ministries, May 15, 2009, https://www.ligonier.org/learn/devotionals/developing-passion-god.

CHAPTER 16: COLLABORATING IN UNITY
1. Philippians 2:2.
2. 1 Corinthians 12:15-19, 21-25.
3. Philippians 2:2, NASB.
4. Matthew 28:19-20.

CHAPTER 17: FOLLOWING A STRATEGY
1. Matthew 6:33.
2. John 13:35.
3. 2 Corinthians 2:12-13.

CHAPTER 18: PUTTING IT ALL TOGETHER
1. "Income Inequality," Greater Louisville Project, accessed December 8, 2023, https://greaterlouisvilleproject.org/factors/income-inequality.
2. Ephesians 4:1.
3. Ephesians 1:3.
4. Ephesians 1:7-9.
5. Matthew 25:34.
6. Ephesians 1:19-20.
7. Ephesians 2:5; 2 Timothy 1:10.
8. 2 Corinthians 5:17; Ephesians 2:13.
9. Ephesians 4:1.
10. Galatians 5:1, NIV.

CHAPTER 19: WHERE IS THE FRUIT?
1. John 15:8.
2. Matthew 21:18-22; Mark 11:12-14, 20-25.
3. Mark 11:12–12:40.
4. John 15:16, NIV.

CHAPTER 20: STORIES OF FRUIT
1. "Haiti's 2022 Hurricane Season," Centre NGO, July 12, 2022, https://www.centrengo.org/2022/07/12/haitis-2022-hurricane-season/.

CHAPTER 23: FRUIT IN AFRICA'S LARGEST SLUM
1. Rosamond Hutt, "These Are the World's Five Biggest Slums," World Economic Forum, October 19, 2016, https://www.weforum.org/agenda/2016/10/these-are-the-worlds-five-biggest-slums.

CHAPTER 24: IMPACT ASSESSMENT STUDY

1. "When Faith Intersects with Development: Searching for Sustainable Impact in the Community Work of Life in Abundance International," Institute for Urban Initiatives (November 2015), 9, 48, https://lifeinabundance .org/wp-content/uploads/2016/04/communityimpactreport.pdf.

2. To read the full text of the Impact Assessment Study, see "When Faith Intersects with Development" at the URL cited in the previous endnote.

CHAPTER 25: THE NEW MISSIONS LANDSCAPE

1. Daniel 2:20-21.

2. Gina A. Zurlo, Todd M. Johnson, and Peter F. Crossing, "World Christianity and Mission 2020: Ongoing Shift to the Global South," *International Bulletin of Mission Research* 44, no. 1 (2020), 8–19, https://doi.org/10.1177 /2396939319880074.

3. Gregory A. Smith, "About Three-in-Ten US Adults Are Now Religiously Unaffiliated," Pew Research Center, December 14, 2021, https://www .pewresearch.org/religion/2021/12/14/about-three-in-ten-u-s-adults -are-now-religiously-unaffiliated/.

4. "Modeling the Future of Religion in America," Pew Research Center, September 13, 2022, https://www.pewresearch.org/religion/2022/09/13 /modeling-the-future-of-religion-in-america/.

5. David McClendon, "Sub-Saharan Africa Will Be Home to Growing Shares of the World's Christians and Muslims," Pew Research Center, April 19, 2017, https://www.pewresearch.org/fact-tank/2017/04/19/sub-saharan-africa-will -be-home-to-growing-shares-of-the-worlds-christians-and-muslims/.

6. Adam Russell Taylor, "Christianity's Future Lies in Africa," *Sojourners*, April 12, 2019, https://sojo.net/articles/christianitys-future-lies-africa.

7. Romans 12:10.

8. G. A. Smith, *Life of William Carey, Shoemaker and Missionary* (Grand Rapids, MI: Christian Classics Ethereal Library, n.d.), 21–22, https://www.ccel .org/ccel/s/smith_geo/carey/cache/carey.pdf.

9. Galatians 2:20.

CHAPTER 26: SHAPING A KINGDOM MINDSET

1. Luke 9:23.

2. Galatians 2:20.

3. Ephesians 2:10.

4. Paul Gericke, *Crucial Experiences in the Life of D. L. Moody* (New Orleans: Insight Press, 1978), 49. Italics in the original.

5. Acts 14:3.

6. Matthew 28:20.

7. 1 Thessalonians 4:1, NLT.

Resources

TRAINING

To participate in LIA's Training of Trainers program, contact us at info@lifeinabundance.org.

BOOKS

Corbett, Steve, and Brian Fikkert. *When Helping Hurts: How to Alleviate Poverty without Hurting the Poor . . . and Yourself.* Chicago: Moody, 2012.

Lupton, Robert D. *Toxic Charity: How Churches and Charities Hurt Those They Help (And How to Reverse It).* New York: HarperOne, 2011.

Muindi, Florence. *The Pursuit of His Calling: Following in Purpose.* Nashville, TN: Integrity Publishers, 2020.

Perbi, Yaw, and Sam Ngugi. *Africa to the Rest: From Mission Field to Mission Force (Again).* Maitland, FL: Xulon Press, 2022.

Polman, Linda. *The Crisis Caravan: What's Wrong with Humanitarian Aid?* New York: Picador, 2010.

Saint, Steve. *The Great Omission: Fulfilling Christ's Commission Completely.* Seattle: YWAM Publishing, 2001.

Schwartz, Timothy T. *Travesty in Haiti: A True Account of Christian Missions, Orphanages, Fraud, Food Aid, and Drug Trafficking.* Charleston, SC: BookSurge Publishing, 2010.

Young, F. Lionel, III. *World Christianity and the Unfinished Task: A Very Short Introduction.* Eugene, OR: Cascade Books, 2021.

About the Authors

FLORENCE MUINDI, MD, is the founder and president of Life In Abundance (LIA) International, a faith-based nonprofit headquartered in Nairobi, Kenya. LIA serves the poor and the vulnerable through partnerships with local indigenous churches, while championing the cause of wholistic transformational development. Dr. Muindi is a medical doctor, an author, and an ordained minister. She and her husband, Dr. Festus Muindi, live in Kenya.

CHARLIE VITTITOW, DMD, AAACD, has served as a dentist, a cofounder of several successful medical equipment companies, and a missions pastor at Southeast Christian Church in Louisville, Kentucky. He delights in seeing local churches around the world strengthened as they receive the skills and biblical insights that make them more relevant in their communities. He find equal delight in enjoying his large family.

JOSEPH AND KATHLEEN SINDORF are award-winning communicators who love to help people touch the hearts of others with clarity and impact. As a veteran international filmmaker and a tenured university communication professor, they love good stories and telling stories well. Learn more about the Sindorfs at wordsmiths.pro.

By purchasing
this book,
you're making
a difference.

For over 60 years, Tyndale has supported ministry

and humanitarian causes around the world through

the work of its foundation. Proceeds from every book sold

benefit the foundation's charitable giving. Thank you

for helping us meet the physical, spiritual, and

educational needs of people everywhere!

 Tyndale | Trusted. For Life.   **tyndale.com/foundation**

And don't forget to do good and to share with those in need. HEBREWS 13:16 (NLT)

CP1665

LIFE IN ABUNDANCE
INTERNATIONAL

Defeat Poverty, Restore Dignity

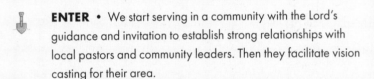

Steps to Sustainable Development

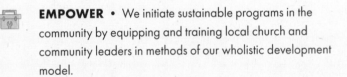

ENTER • We start serving in a community with the Lord's guidance and invitation to establish strong relationships with local pastors and community leaders. Then they facilitate vision casting for their area.

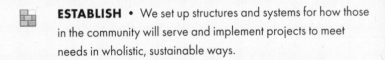

EMPOWER • We initiate sustainable programs in the community by equipping and training local church and community leaders in methods of our wholistic development model.

ESTABLISH • We set up structures and systems for how those in the community will serve and implement projects to meet needs in wholistic, sustainable ways.

EXPAND • We strengthen existing programs to equip other churches as the impact of the work reaches surrounding communities.

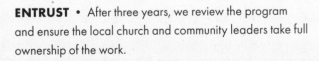

ENTRUST • After three years, we review the program and ensure the local church and community leaders take full ownership of the work.

Contact Us!

EMAIL INFO@LIFEINABUNDANCE.ORG
OR VISIT WWW.LIFEINABUNDANCE.ORG

CP1988